Intervallic Ear Training for Musicians

Steve Prosser

Intervallic Ear Training for Musicians

Steve Prosser

advance music

© 2010 Advance Music

All Rights Reserved.

No parts of this publication may be reproduced, stored in a retrieval system,
or transmitted, in any form or by any means, electronic, mechanical,
photocopying, recording, or otherwise, without prior
written permission of Advance Music.

International Copyright Secured.

Cover Art: Schultz + Schultz Mediengestaltung, Wien, Austria

Layout and music typesetting: T. Max Zentawer

Production: Veronika Gruber

Order No. 16310

ISBN 3-89221-107-8

Table Of Contents

Preface 6

Reference Chapter. 7

Chapter 1 · 2nds 16

Chapter 2 · 3rds 31

Chapter 3 · 4ths & 5ths 46

Chapter 4 · Tritones 61

Chapter 5 · 6ths 74

Chapter 6 · 7ths 89

Chapter 7 · Dictation 104

About the Author. 122

Preface

Why Intervallic Studies?

When studying ear training systems such as movable-Do solfegio, you focus on learning and memorizing relationships between pitches. Those relationships are predicated upon a sense of *resolution*. Thus, the function Sol is Sol because it theoretically resolves to Do – at least that's how you learn to form and memorize the sound. What if Sol has no sound of resolution to Do? The obvious answer is that Sol would no longer be Sol. It would merely be a pitch without a relationship!

Losing a sense of Do, however, is a phenomenon that all ear training students discover at one point or another in their studies; Losing Do often happens in advanced chromatic melodies or in melodies which have quickly shifting key centers. Indeed, some music entirely defies a sense of key. For these melodic situations it is often necessary to employ a hearing technique to complement movable-Do solfege. Hearing *by interval* is that complement.

Hearing by interval is not as easy as it sounds and, indeed, many students find interval study to be most difficult. The reason for that difficulty is not readily apparent. Many ear training and solfege method books contain interval studies, but those studies are usually *contextual* interval studies. Sol down to Do, for example, is said to be a Perfect 5th interval; and while that is entirely true, that particular example does not necessarily prove *intrinsic* interval hearing. Such contextual interval studies are fine for learning interval *theory* but are not particularly useful for learning the primary sound of intervals in a way that allows their practical use in reading or composing. Simply put, you must learn and memorize the sound of each interval *as it is of itself*, usable in any musical context.

The interval studies in "Intervallic Ear Training for Musicians" require that you build intervals by measuring and memorizing their musical sizes *without* the context of tonality. Thus, the interval studies may be said to be *atonal*. Now, the term atonal is one that often sends a shudder through ear training students, but there is really nothing to fear. Interval study, when approached with the proper technique, is not more difficult than any other musical endeavor.

Learning and memorizing the sound of musical intervals is a worthy and necessary endeavor for a musician, and you will find that interval study not only creates a more independent and competent musical mind, but broadens your aesthetic appreciation by providing a primary understanding of musical architecture.

Steve Prosser

Boston, Massachusetts

November, 2009

Reference Chapter

Steps in music reading and singing:

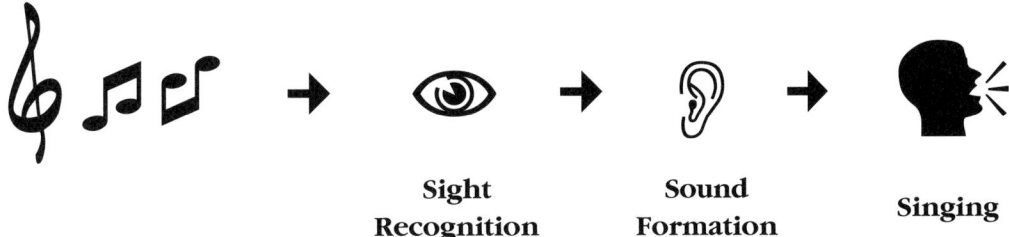

Sight Recognition

The goal of sight recognition is to make your identification of intervals fluid and intuitive. You must first make sure that you can identify each interval by sight before singing. This is most effectively done by comparing each set. For example comparing minor 2^{nds} to major 2^{nds}. Simply set a reasonable tempo (one in which you can do the identification but are challenged by the tempo). Then *say* the interval name out loud. Take note of the intervals that cause sight recognition problems – take a careful look at each problem – and then repeat the sight recognition example you have chosen.

You can do sight recognition in the "Preparatory" section of each Chapter. But first read on!

Sound Formation

Sound formation is the memory response to the music that you see and recognize. This process is sometimes called using the "internal" or "inner" ear. Sound formation, usually treated as an intuitive function in ear training study is, rather, the most important developmental step in the assimilation and long-term memorization of intervals. Indeed, working on your sound formation accomplishes the important effect of "making your musical brain an instrument itself."

Simply put sound formation is accomplished, in the initial stages, by putting space between the singing of each pitch. During this time, your brain translates the interval that you recognize, produces a memory of the sound, and sets your vocal chords ready to sing (this is called muscular memory).

Sound formation eliminates note guessing and lessens the need to make pitch adjustments during singing. In this way, sound formation hastens accuracy and long-term memorization of each interval.

Singing

First, the obvious. Once you have recognized the interval, formed the sound you are ready to sing. Give yourself a reference pitch. A piano is fine, or you can use a more transportable device such as a tuning fork or pitch wheel. *But, avoid playing the intervals on your reference source.* You are not learning to match pitches, but rather build intervals. If you play the intervals before you sing them, you will never learn them. If you play the reference instrument after each note you sing, you will inevitably come to rely on the instrument. Remember, your goal is to develop the sound internally without external help. The only appropriate time to play the instrument is when you give yourself a reference note or when you check yourself at the end of an example. However, if you do the technique properly, you will know whether you are correct at the end of the example. Try the following example:

- Play a "C" on your reference instrument.
- Sing the "C", concentrating on your intonation (use "la" or "doo").
- Stop.
- Look at the next pitch, "B" and identify the interval from "C", a minor 2nd.
- Form the sound in your head. Take as long as you need for this.
- Sing the "B", concentrating on your intonation (sing a long tone and listen carefully to yourself).
- Stop and check your intonation on your reference instrument.
- If you are sharp or flat, go back and repeat the entire process until you become confident of the two notes.
- Repeat this process from "B" to "A#".
- Finally, sing the entire exercise.

The Basic Idea

The goal of interval study is to measure and memorize the size of each melodic interval accurately. The most effective way to undertake that task is to start with the smallest interval, the minor 2nd, and work upwards through the larger intervals. That is how the exercises in this book proceed. In order to begin, however, you have to have a confident sense of the sound of the smallest interval, the minor 2nd. It is the smallest interval used in typical Western music and you must be confident that you can build it from your memory. You must establish this confidence before you begin because the rest of the study, using additive construction or *building blocks*, is based on your initial ability to hear and sing the minor 2nd. The following two examples will help to prepare you for interval study in the first chapter.

To help you reinforce the minor 2nd, the first interval exercise is the chromatic scale. You will recognize this scale from other melodic studies. For the purpose of intervallic study you should practice the scale *without* solfege; just sing on "La" or some similar syllable. After giving yourself the reference pitch of "C", sing the pitch, concentrating on your intonation. Then stop. Look at the next pitch, C♯. After hearing the pitch, sing it, concentrating on the size of the interval motion you just made and on your intonation. Continue this process through the rest of the scale, up and down. The next exercise utilizes a scale for comparison, the whole-tone scale.

The intervals in this scale are twice as large as in the chromatic scale previously discussed. That information is important to you. You can use what you already know (the size of a minor 2nd) to build a major 2nd. Notice that in the scale the second note, C♯, is darkened – that note designates a *building block*.

The Building Block Technique

A *building block* is a smaller interval used to bridge to a larger interval. Its purpose is to help you form the sound of the larger interval. Using the exercise above, give yourself a reference pitch, sing the first note, a "C." As before, make sure of your good intonation and then stop. Look at the building block note, C♯. Sing that pitch when you hear it. Look at the next pitch, D. Sing it when you hear it. Now sing back to "C." Repeat this sequence of notes over and over until you begin to sense the size of the larger interval C to D. When you are sure of that sound, stop singing the building block note and repeat the sequence C to D.

This technique will reinforce the sound of the major second interval. You should utilize this building block technique throughout the whole tone scale when you are unsure of the sound and size of a major 2nd.

The Interval (Atonal) Problems

In each chapter you will find exercises designated as atonal problems. These exercises address the interval problems with which most musicians have difficulty, i.e., ones that are tonally ambiguous or lack a sense of resolution. These exercises are routinely followed by longer exercises which reinforce the atonal problems. The beginning exercises are presented without a time signature and without rhythm. You should practice these exercises utilizing the following technique:

1. Sing the first note, concentrating on pitch and stop.
2. Identify the interval to the next note.
3. Hear the interval in your head (Sing a building block if you get stuck).
4. Sing the pitch, concentrating on pitch and stop.

The Mastery Exercises

Following the atonal problems and the related exercises for each interval set, there follows so-called combined studies which add the difficulties of time signature and rhythm. The goal of these studies is to gain interval mastery and to demonstrate practical interval usage. You will notice that the rhythmic difficulty in these combined interval studies is somewhat simple to start. This rhythmic presentation allows you to integrate the interval problems with rhythm and time more slowly.

Please remember that your main concern in these exercises should be the accurate hearing and singing of each interval; Thus, the *setting of tempo* is once again extremely important to your success. You must pick a tempo that allows you to *know* that you are singing the correct interval – it doesn't matter how slow that is! Take each exercise as it comes – you will be able to sing some faster than others. Remember that, while speed does demonstrate mastery, your primary concern is with building and memorizing accurate interval sizes. After finding a good practice tempo, remember to conduct as you sing each exercise.

Although the rhythmic element, as mentioned, is less difficult in the beginning studies, you may find that you need or want to break down the components in some exercises. You can utilize a "Steps" technique similar to the one outlined in the melodic studies reference section:

Steps Technique

Step 1: Identify the interval

If you are having trouble with figuring out what intervals you are looking at, try the following: Set a slow pulse on the metronome. *Disregarding rhythm and pitch*, say the intervals out loud. You will be able to identify problematic interval sight recognition in this way.

Step 2: Do the rhythm alone

It is impractical to try to say the interval size as you do the rhythm given their multi-syllabic nature. So, set a slow tempo on the metronome and say the rhythm, taking note of problem areas.

Step 3: Sing the intervals alone

Without rhythm or time, sing each interval. Put space between each sung interval. Use a *building block* when you need to. This step is particularly useful when you are having trouble with a particular intervallic motion.

Step 4: Sing the example

Again, using an effective practice tempo, sing the example. If you find that you still have a particular problem go back to the related Step and work out the recognition, rhythm, or interval problem.

When you feel that you have mastered an exercise at the slower practice tempo, gradually work your way up to the suggested tempo of the exercise. Finally, you should begin to feel that you are singing music (i.e. with some sense of musical appreciation) not just an exercise!

Progression of Studies

As mentioned, the intervallic studies utilize additive construction beginning with the smallest interval, the minor 2nd. Note that each new interval study also makes use of the interval(s) previously studied. The chapter progression of studies is as follows: minor and major 2nds, minor and major 3rds, perfect 4ths and perfect 5ths, tritones, minor and major 6ths, minor and major 7ths, and finally combined studies.

Visualization-Improvisation

Visualization-improvisation is a supplemental exercise to help reinforce the intervallic reading studies. The goal of *visualization-improvisation*, as the name suggests, is to see in your head pitches on a musical instrument as you sing melodies of your own creation. The preferred instrument for this exercise is a piano because of its common use in all aspects of music and because the brain can easily visualize the black and white keys, but your instrument (the frets of a guitar, or sax fingerings) or even an image of musical notation may be used if you can visualize it with more clarity.

The results of extensive practice in visualization-improvisation are profound. One of the primary goals of ear training is to make the musical mind a competent, secure, and flexible instrument *in and of itself*. The ability of that musical mind to internally create or interpret external musical sound is a result of accomplishing that goal. That ability has important ramifications for musical use: the skill to envision music as it is composed leaving only a final task of physical notation, the capacity to see printed music and to hear that music without playing the music on another instrument, and the proficiency to hear played or recorded music and to understand its shape and form, possibly to the extent of seeing in the mind's eye the notes as they are played and heard. These are, most certainly, worthwhile abilities to seek through study. Most importantly, though, these are abilities which *can* be enhanced through visualization-improvisation.

How To Do Visualization-Improvisation

The keyboard on the next page is for demonstrating the visualization-improvisation technique. Look at the keyboard and then close your eyes – try to see the keyboard. Run up and down the chromatic notes in your mind from C up to a higher C. If you can "see" all the notes as you go then you are ready to proceed with the exercises. If you decide to utilize another visualization device, try the same experiment with your eyes closed. No matter the instrument you choose to see, you have to decide if your sense of the structure of the instrument as your mind sees it is vivid enough to add the difficulties of function and pitch. If you cannot yet visualize any instrument, then you should utilize the keyboard provided in the book and use it in conjunction with your exercises. When you feel more confident about the structure of the keyboard, you can experiment with your eyes closed. This will not take as long as you probably think, so don't get frustrated with the process in the early stages.

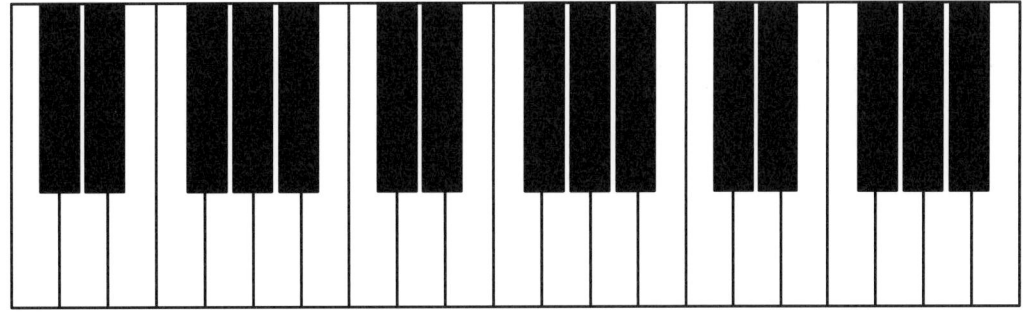

As mentioned, the visualization-improvisation exercise is meant to compliment your intervallic studies. When should you start trying the exercises? The best answer is: start when you begin to feel confident with a certain component of your studies. For instance, in the early chapters of the book, you work with minor and major 2nds. When you start to feel confident about the interval problems in the chapter you should begin to do visualization-improvisation. Your early success or failure with the visualization-improvisation exercise will be based on your carefully following the outlined technique which follows:

Visualization-Improvisation Technique

The best way to begin with visualization-improvisation is to try singing without a tempo – just to feel your way around the keyboard. For this example let's use one of the minor/major 2nd problems, C up a whole step to D, then down a half-step to D♭. First, give yourself a reference note of C. Close your eyes and see the note and sing it, saying the note name. Once you are satisfied with your pitch, stop. Then, with your eyes closed, see the next ascending note D. Get the pitch in your head and when you are sure of the pitch, sing the note name. Then stop. Continue in this fashion to the D♭. Make sure each note is visualized on the keyboard or your instrument of choice. The more vivid your "sight" the better. This vividness will improve dramatically with practice.

Once you understand the technique of visualization-improvisation, you should begin to improvise melodies of your own choice. Make sure to concentrate on the interval problems as you create your improvisation. In other words, you "improvise" using the interval problem sets, but with the freedom to begin on any pitch and in any sequence. Disciplining yourself in this way will provide you with the most benefit in permanently learning the interval problems.

Moving Ahead with Visualization-Improvisation

There are some logical variations to the visualization-improvisation exercises as outlined. As you get more secure with visualization-improvisation, you can drop the restis from your performance, or you can improvise in a rhythmic context over a metronome pulse. You may also want to practice visualization-improvisation without any metronome pulse and work toward more freely phrased melodies. You might want to work on visualization of the staff, utilizing treble and bass clefs. These latter type of exercises suggest one of the practical uses of melodic visualization discussed earlier – the ability to see as you compose.

Indeed, it is hoped that you will find visualization-improvisation both the most ultimately practical and aesthetically meaningful musical exercises that you will undertake in the study of intervals. This is an activity that you can take with you – as you walk down the street, in your car, sitting quietly in a room. And it is an activity which will help prepare you for the working tasks of music: Composition, improvisation, reading, and understanding what is heard. Thus, you are strongly encouraged to make visualization-improvisation a significant part of your daily interval work – you will find it well worth the effort.

Dictation

The CD that accompanies this book contains dictation exercises that will reinforce both the accuracy of your interval perception as well as the clarity of your mental music imaging. The following explanations relate to the various types of dictation you will encounter:

1. **Interval lines:** These exercises start with a single pitch and then add one note at a time; these exercises focus, naturally, on building interval problems. So, as with your visualization-improvisation, memorizing the various interval problems will assist you in the dictation. The goal of this exercise is to translate the sound, through interval identification, and to visualize and memorize the notes as they are added. A reference pitch will be given on the CD. After each note set is played, pause the CD and carefully sing back the line; remember to use the same sing-pause-sing technique as you use for the interval studies. When each exercise is completed, and only then, write down the notes and compare them to the answer provided in the back of the book. If you have trouble with the exercise, repeat it more slowly with more repetition of singing and visualization.

2. **Duets:** These exercises are, simply put, point-on-point duets. They have no specified rhythm. The goal here is to translate, sing and memorize each line. It is usually easier to start with the top line, but you can decide. The reference pitch will be given and then the entire duet will be played. Translate each line in its entirety before writing it down. You should be able to sing and see the line before transcription.

3. **Harmonies:** The goal of these exercises is to hear the vertical interval structure of the chord. Each chord will be vertically constructed from the intervals of the particular chapter. So, the 2^{nds} Chapter will only have seconds in the voicing from note to note. If you hear something else, listen again! Repeat each voicing as often as you need to hear and see each note. When you are sure of the harmony, write it down.

4. **Three-Note Chord Sets:** These exercises are, as with the duets, point-on-point exercise with no specified rhythm. The goal here, however is a little different. Instead of linear memorization, you must try to memorize the vertical note changes. This is quite difficult and you may find that you have to repeat each exercise many times before you can accurately translate the notes. The reference pitches will be given for the three vertical notes, i.e. the chord. Then the first chord will move back and forth between the second chord. After a number of repetitions (during which time it is hoped you will recognize which notes change and where they go), the second chord will move back and forth between the third chord and so on. After the entire exercise is completed, you may write it down and check the answer in the book. These exercises will begin with just a few chords and gradually increase to eight chords. Work at your own pace and don't worry if you need to repeat a number of times. Remember, you are training your mind to be the musical instrument – no easy task!

CHAPTER 1 · 2nds

Preparatory Exercises

The first intervals you will study are the smallest – 2nds (please refer to the reference section in the beginning of this book). The following preparatory exercises should be used for *Sight Recognition* purposes and then to master the sing-pause-sing technique outlined in the reference section. This work will prepare you to move on to the *Interval Problem Exercises* that follow.

Note: For purposes of this study, augmented unisons and diminished 3rds will be noted as 2nds.

Minor 2nds

CHAPTER 1 • 2nds

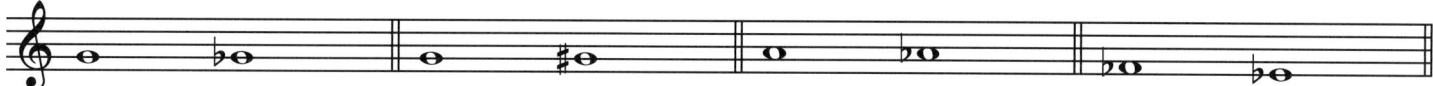

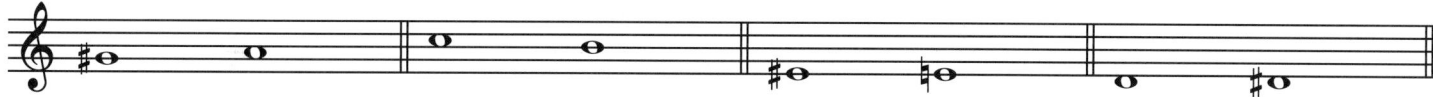

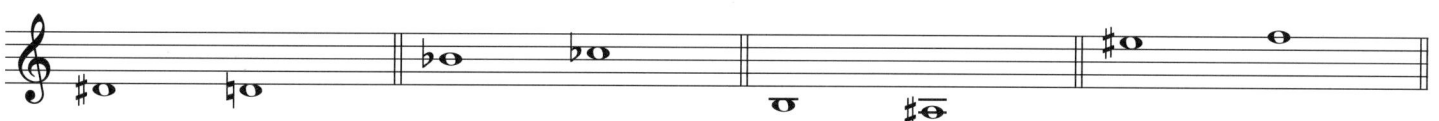

Major 2nds

In working on major 2nds, you will find it useful to employ your memory of the minor 2nd as a *Building Block*. Utilize the technique outlined in the following example.

Using the Building Block:

- Play a "C" reference pitch
- Sing the note, check intonation and stop
- Look at the next pitch, "B" natural
- Form the sound, then sing
- Look at the next pitch, "B♭"
- Form the sound and sing
- Work back and forth between the 3 pitches
- Become aware of the outer interval, "C" down to "B♭"
- Stop singing the middle note "B" and sing
- "C" down to "B♭".

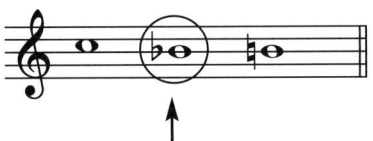

The building block, B natural

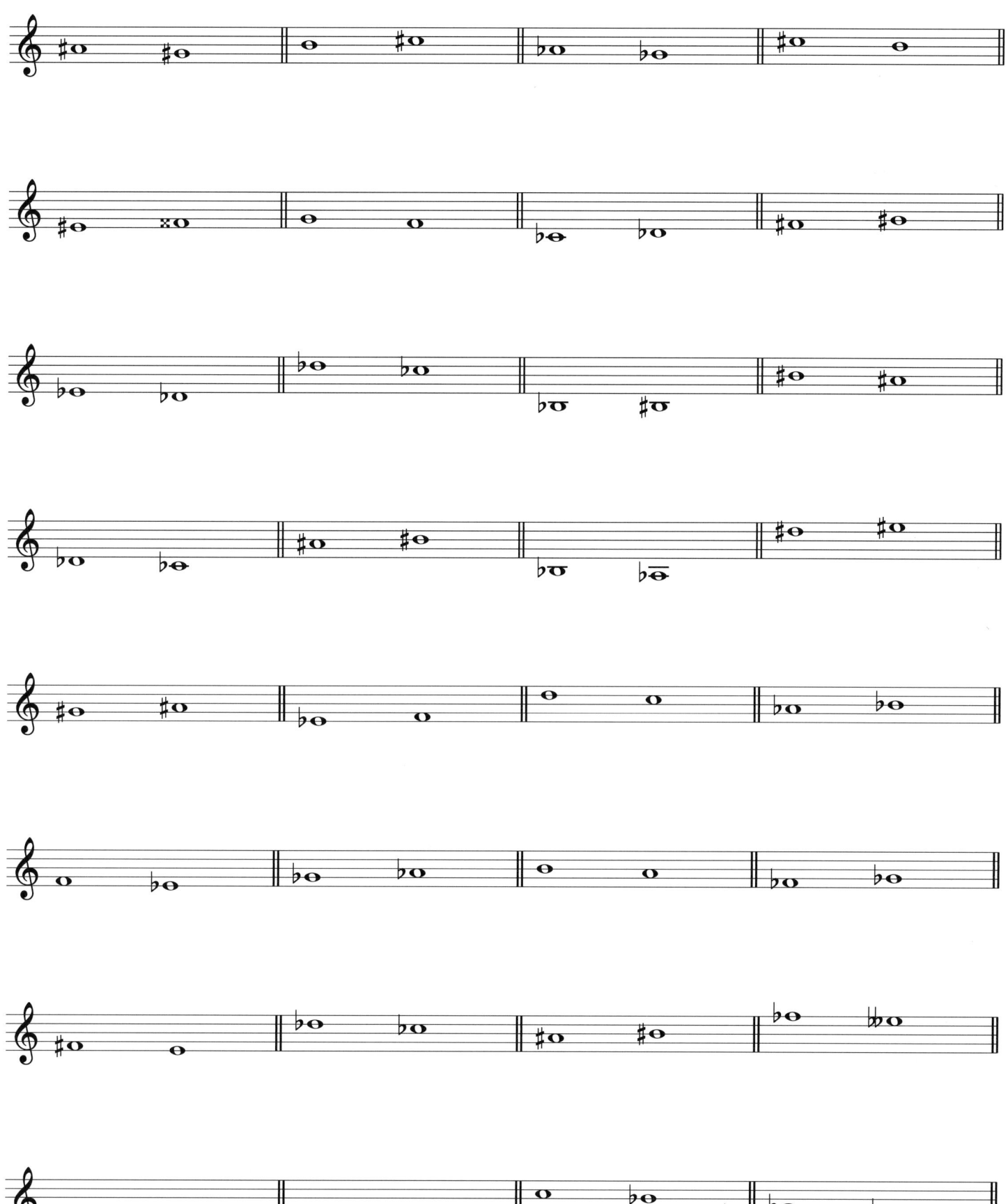

INTERVALLIC EAR TRAINING

Three-Note Sets

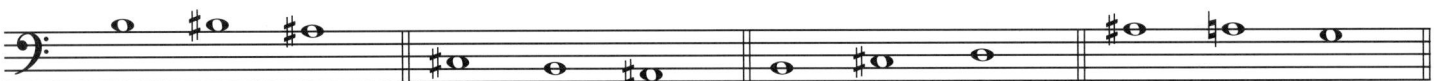

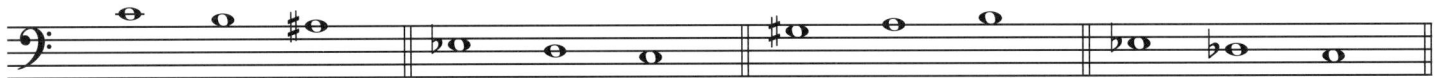

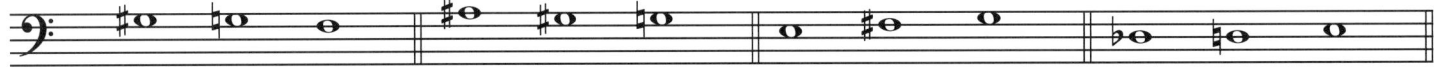

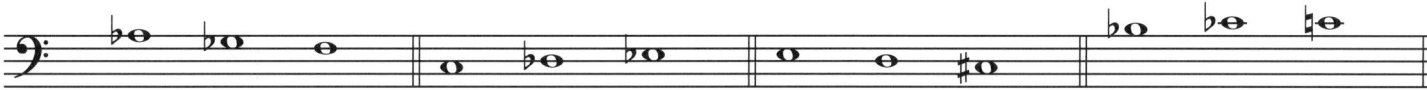

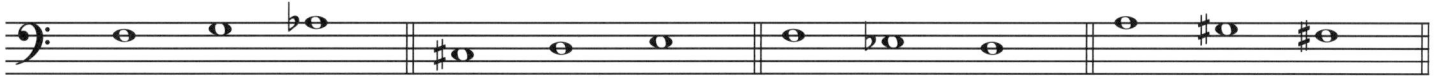

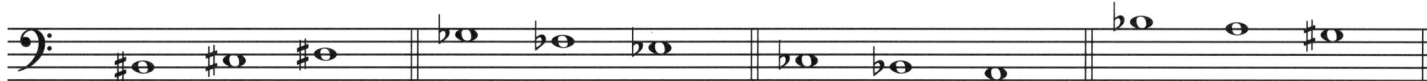

Interval Problem Exercises

The following three problem sets should be mastered one at a time before moving on to the "Open Exercises". Remember to utilize the sing-pause-sing technique that is described in the Reference section. It is essential to your progress that you do so.

Chromatic Tones

Whole Tones

Changing Tones

You can now begin regular Visualization-Improvisation work.

Work the following note-sets back and forth in direction.

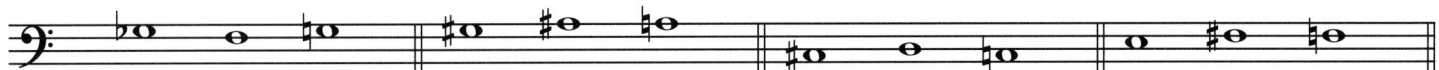

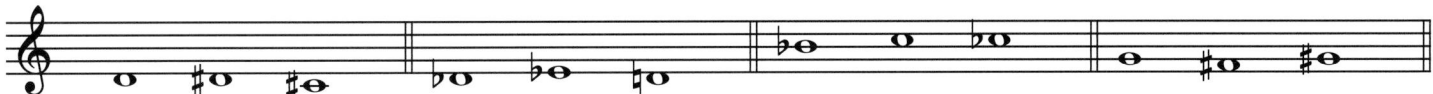

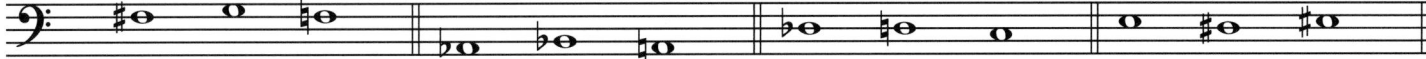

INTERVALLIC EAR TRAINING

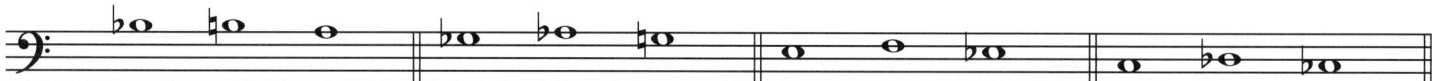

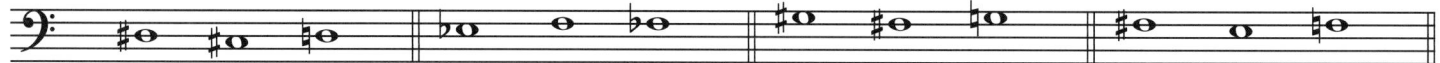

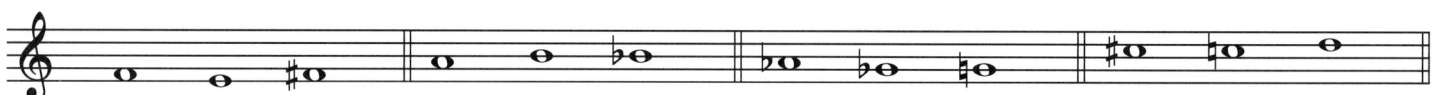

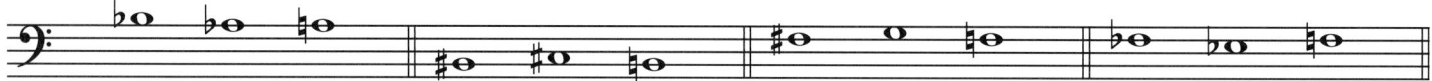

You can now begin regular Dictation (consult the Reference Section).

CHAPTER 1 • 2nds

Open Pages

On the following pages you can begin to work on longer exercises. Note that these pages utilize all of the Interval Problem Sets. Practice until you can sing each whole page between checking. Use the sing-pause-sing technique!

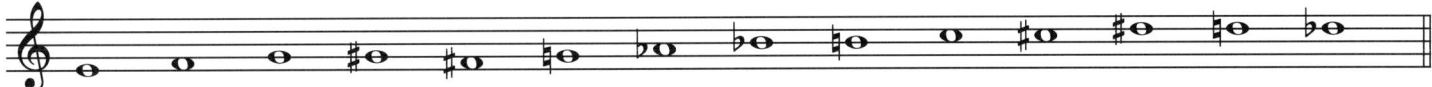

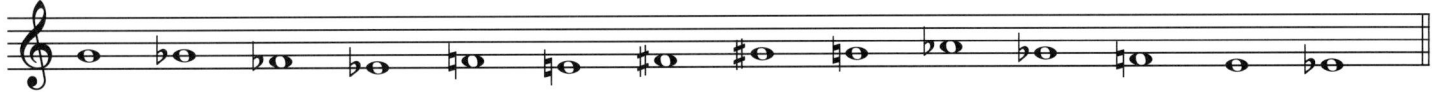

INTERVALLIC EAR TRAINING

Mastery Exercises

These integrated exercises should be begun with a slow tempo (please review the Reference Chapter). You should sing melodies as music – not exercises, i.e. you can stop the sing-pause-sing method and sing the melodies smoothly. If you find that the melodies, at any tempo, are too hard, go back and work on the problems.

INTERVALLIC EAR TRAINING

Etudes

The tempos indicated are performance goals, so don't begin there. Instead, choose a tempo that challenges you to know that you are singing the right notes.

CHAPTER 2 • 3rds

Preparatory Exercises

The next interval set you will study is 3rds. The Preparatory Exercises for minor and major 3rds should be used for Sight Recognition purposes and then to master the sing-pause-sing technique. The following Building Block example will help you use what you already know - 2nds - to help you build 3rds.

Using the Building Block:

- Play a "A" reference pitch
- Sing the note, check intonation and stop
- Look at the next pitch, "B" natural
- Form the sound, then sing
- Look at the next pitch, "C"
- Form the sound and sing
- Work back and forth between the 3 pitches
- Become aware of the outer interval, "A" down to "C"

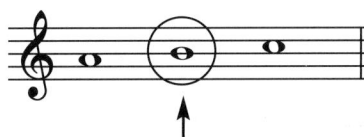

The building block, B natural

Minor 3rds

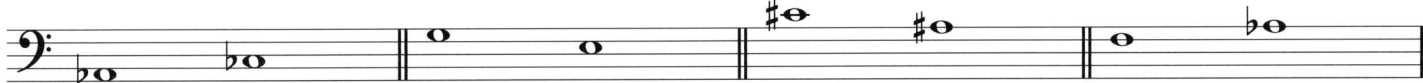

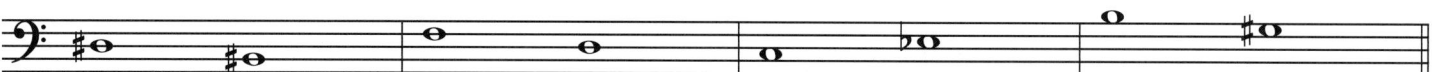

Major 3rds

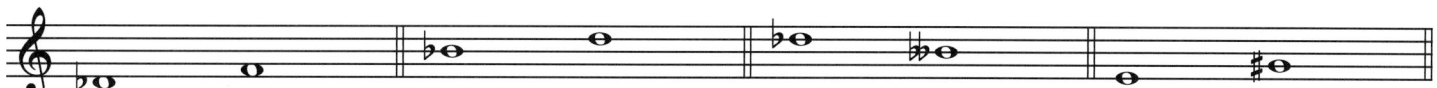
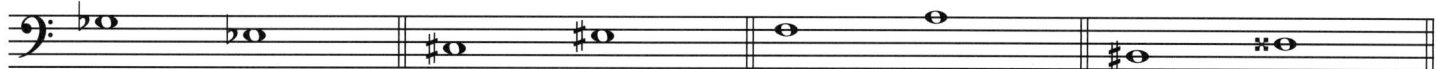
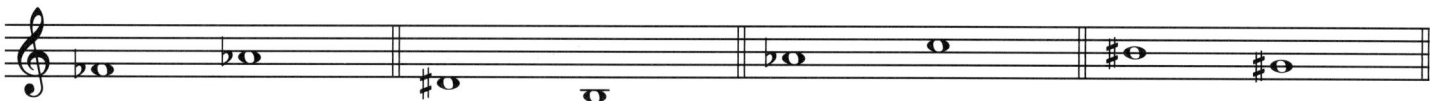
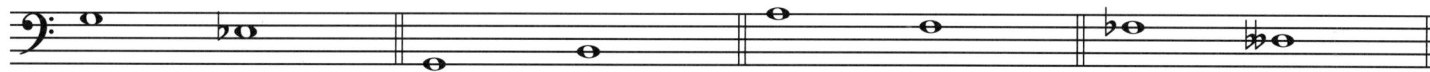

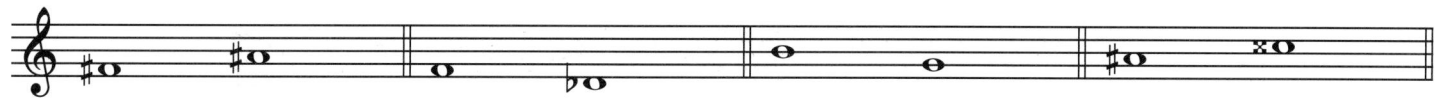
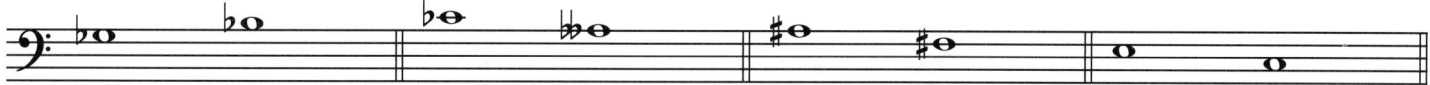

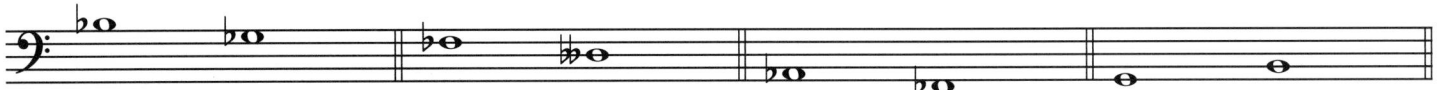

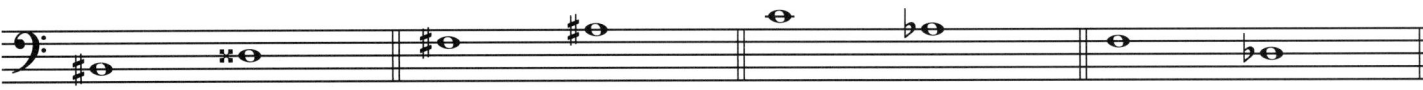
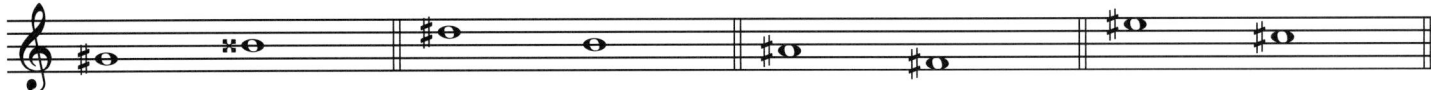
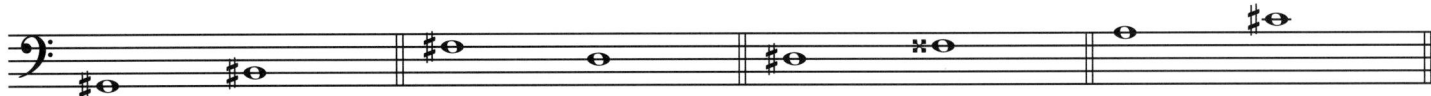
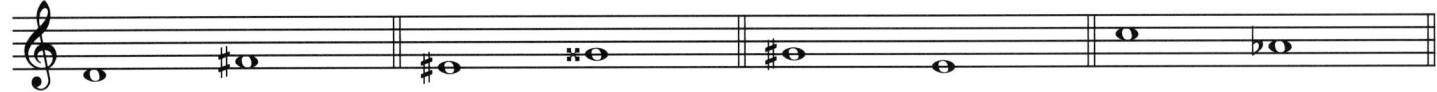
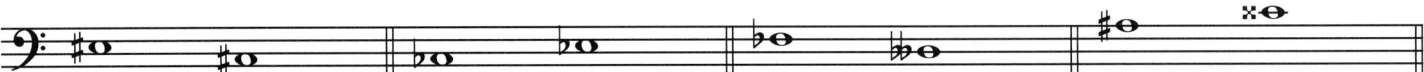

Three-Note Sets

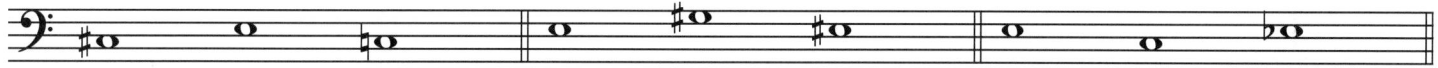

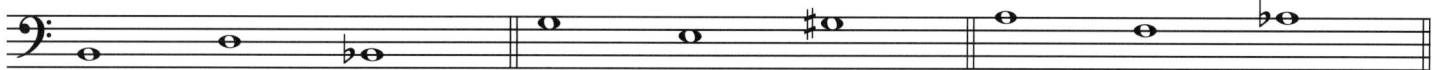

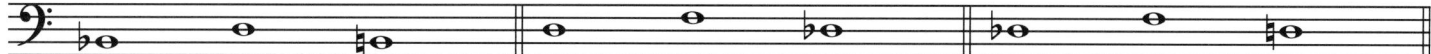

INTERVALLIC EAR TRAINING

Interval Problem Exercises

The following three problem sets should be mastered one at a time before moving on to the "Open Exercises". Remember to utilize the sing-pause-sing technique that is described in the Reference section. It is essential to your progress that you do so.

Also remember to use a *Building Block* whenever you need to.

Minor 3rds

For example, use a "G" as a *Building Block* between "F" and "A♭".

Major 3rds

3rds and minor 2nds

You can now begin regular Visualization-Improvisation work. Use all of the problem sets from all chapters that you have studied.

2nds and 3rds Problem Sets

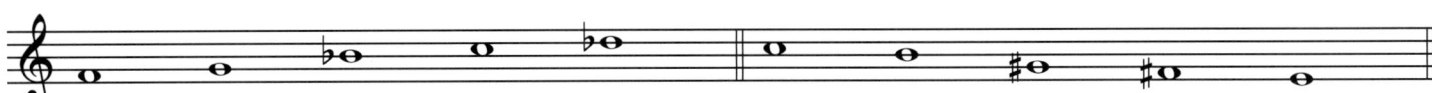

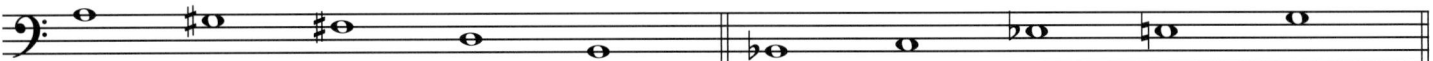

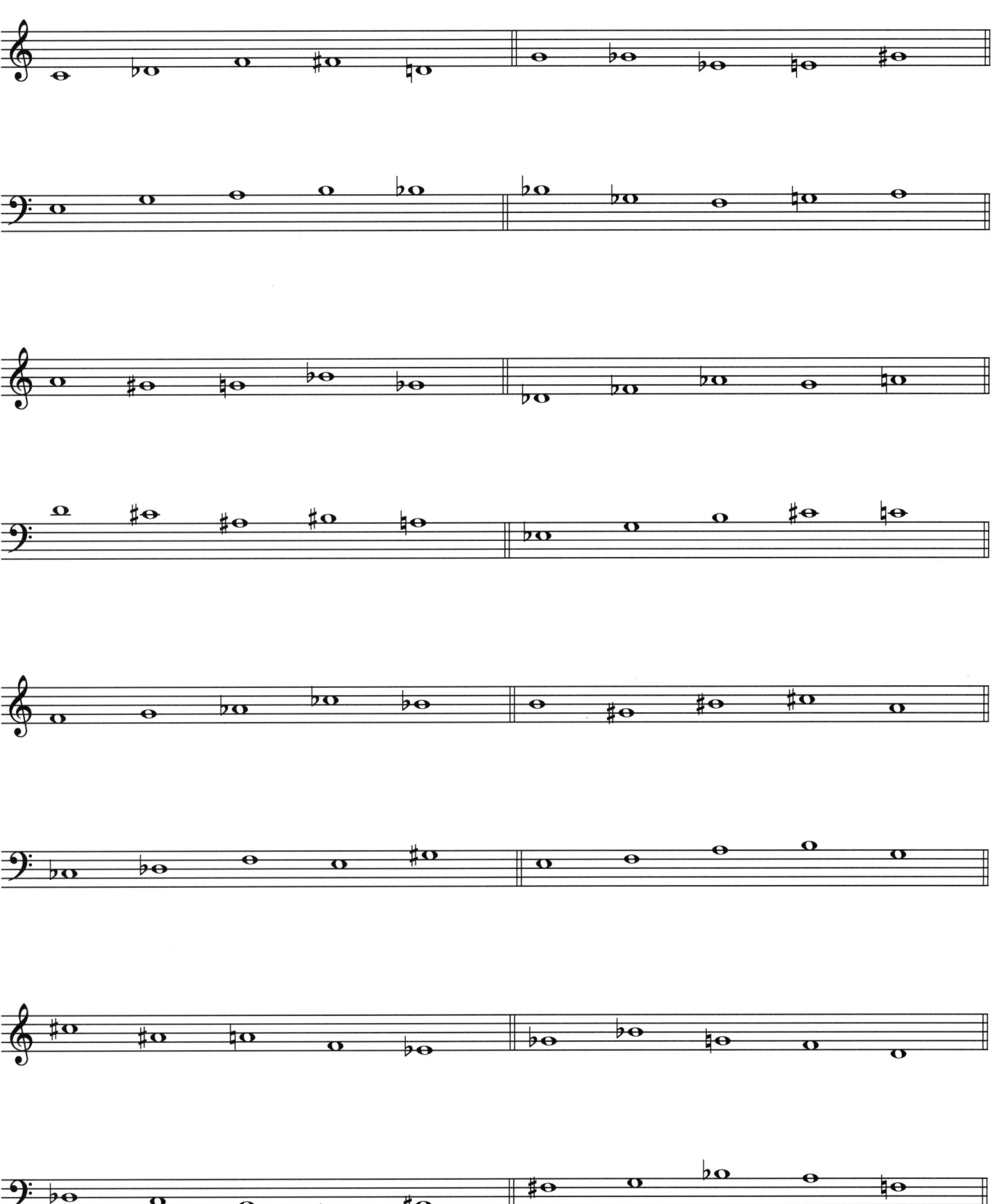

You can now begin Dictation (consult the Reference Section).

2nds and 3rds - Open Pages

On the following pages you can begin to work on longer exercises. Note that these pages utilize all of the Interval Problem Sets. Practice until you can sing each whole example between checking. Use the sing-pause-sing technique!

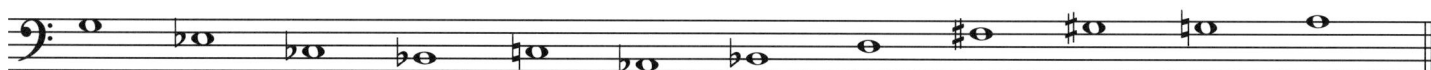

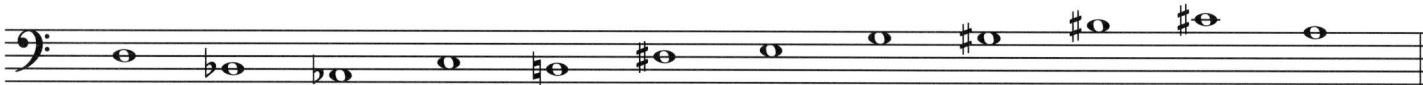

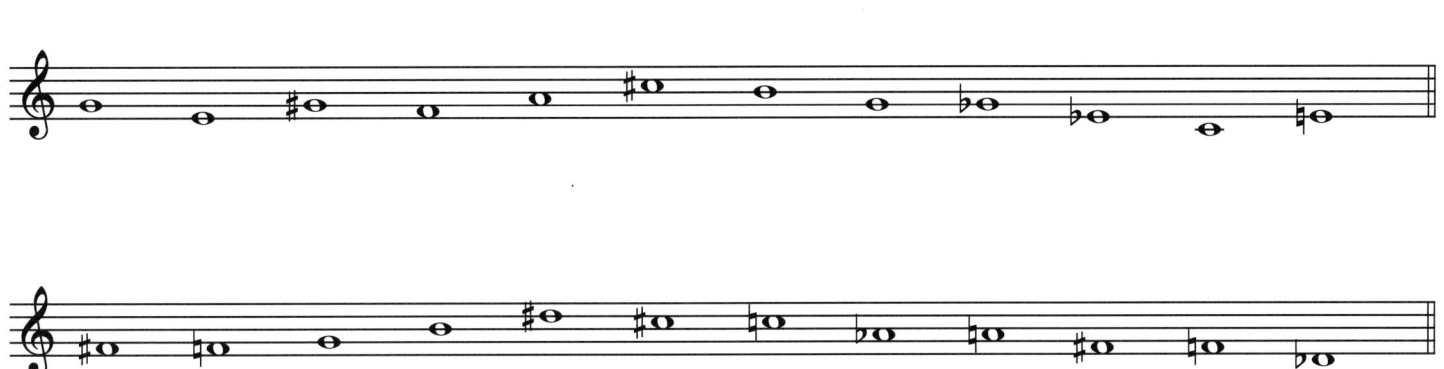

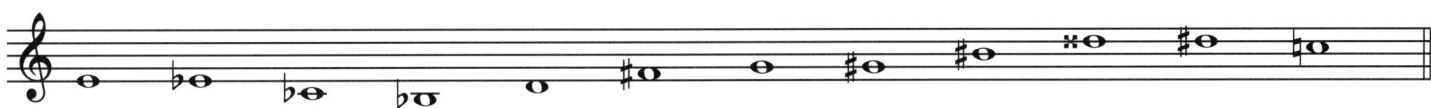

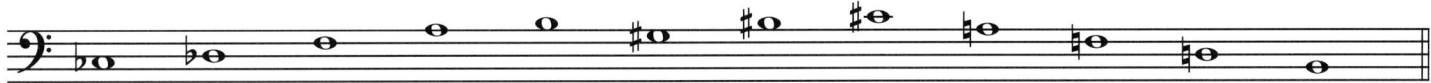
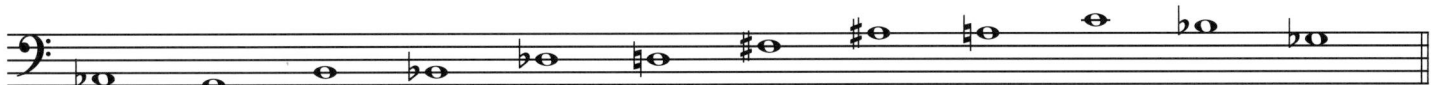

Mastery Exercises

These integrated exercises should be begun with a slow tempo (please review the Reference Chapter). You should sing melodies as music – not exercises, i.e. you can stop the sing-pause-sing method and sing the melodies smoothly. If you find that the melodies, at any tempo, are too hard, go back and work on the problems.

CHAPTER 2 • 3rds

43

Etudes

The tempos indicated are performance goals, so don't begin there.
Instead, choose a tempo that challenges you to know that you are singing
the right notes.

CHAPTER 3 • 4ths & 5ths

Preparatory Exercises

The next interval set you will study contains Perfect 4ths and 5ths. The Preparatory Exercises for these intervals should be used for *Sight Recognition* purposes and then to master the sing-pause-sing technique. The following Building Block example will use intervals that you already know to help you build 4ths and 5ths.

Using the Building Block

- Play an "F" reference pitch
- Sing the note, check intonation and stop
- Look at the next pitch, "A" natural
- Form the sound, then sing
- Look at the next pitch, "B♭"
- Form the sound and sing
- Work back & forth between the 3 pitches
- Become aware of the outer interval, "F" up to "B♭"
- Continuing, stop singing the middle note "A"

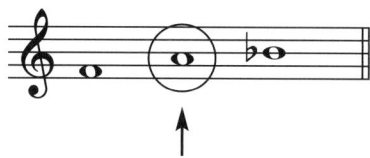

The building block, A natural

Perfect 4ths

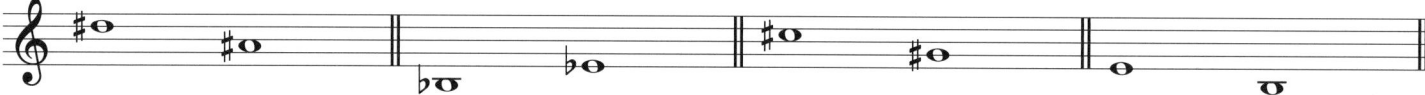

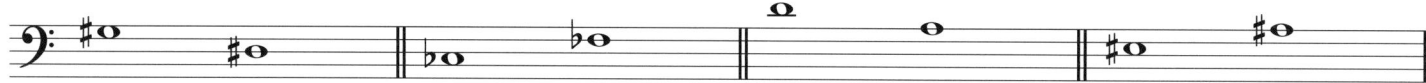

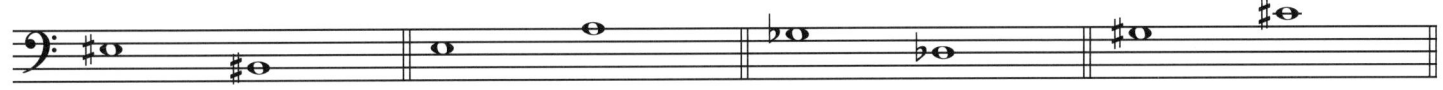
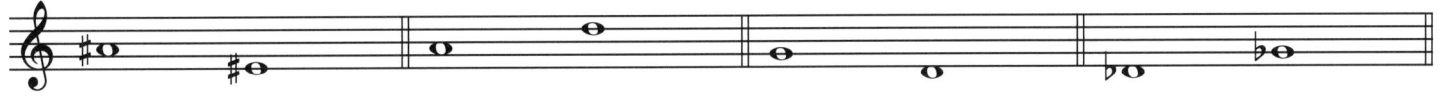
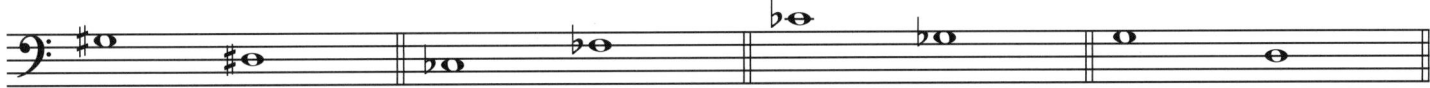

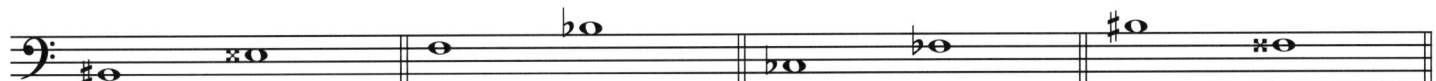

Perfect 5ths

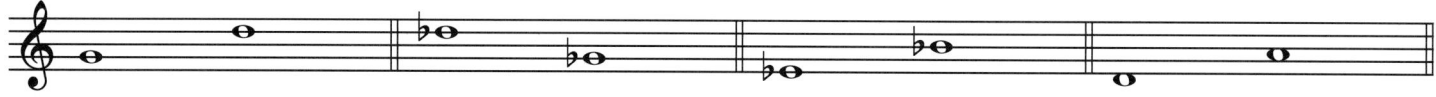

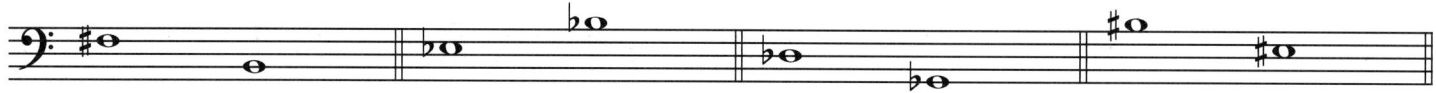

CHAPTER 3 • 4ths & 5ths

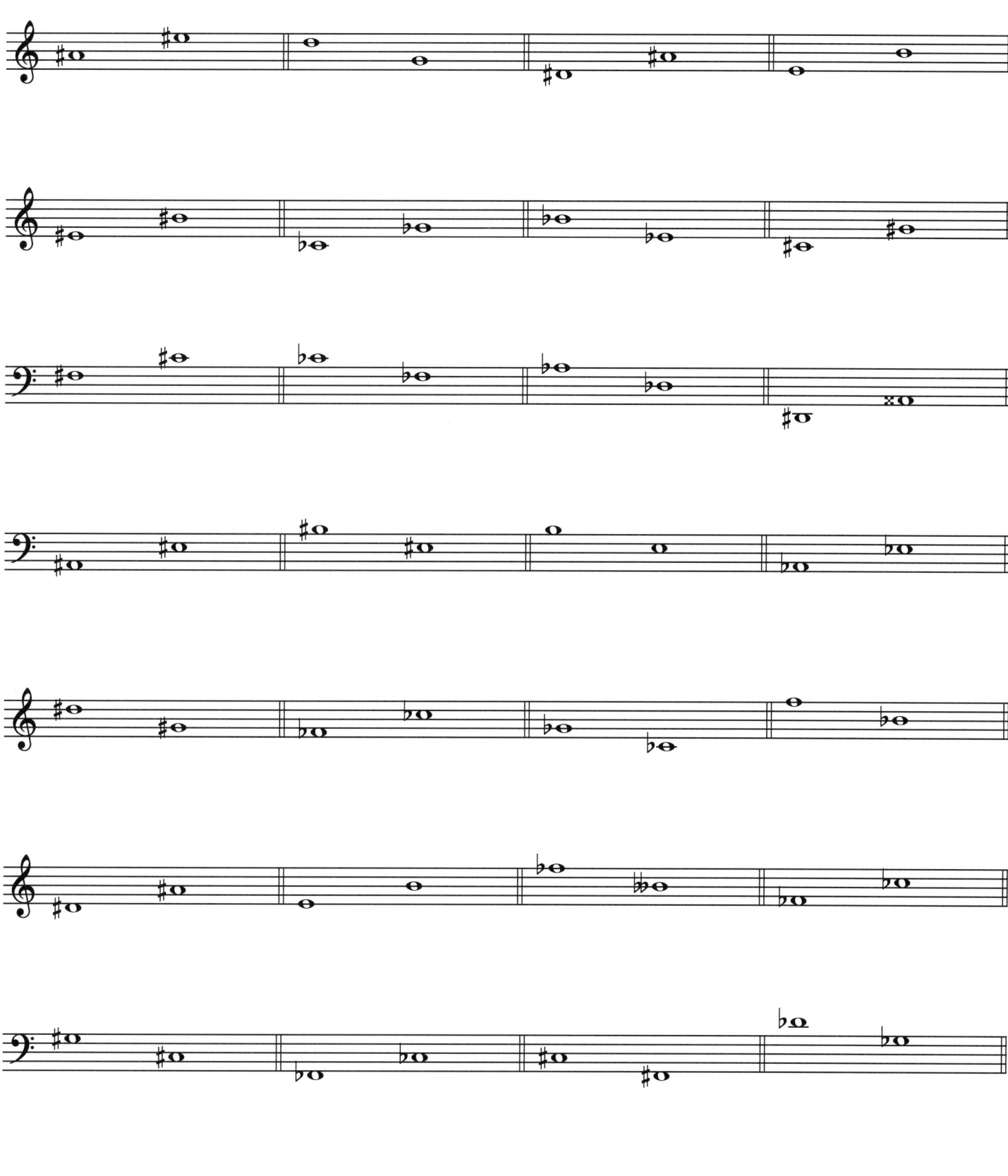

49

Three-Note Sets

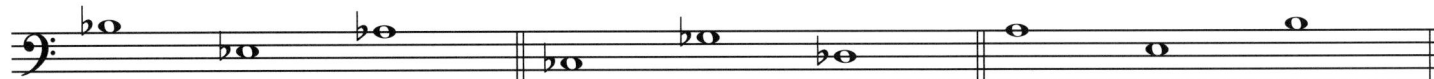

CHAPTER 3 • 4ths & 5ths

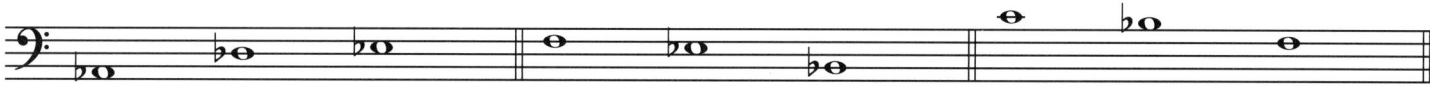
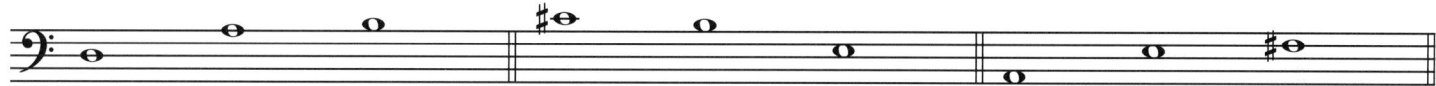

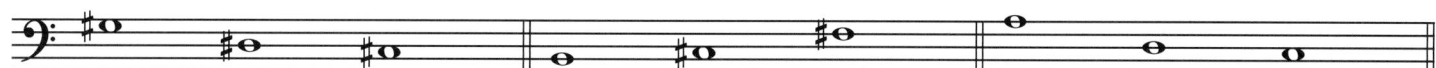

51

Interval Problem Exercises

The following three problem sets should be mastered one at a time before moving on to the Open Exercises. Remember to utilize the sing-pause-sing technique that is described in the Reference section. It is essential to your progress that you do so.

Also remember to use a *Building Block* whenever you need to.

Perfect 4ths

Consecutive Perfect 4ths (both directions)

Perfect 5ths

Consecutive Perfect 5ths (both directions)

4ths, 5ths and minor 2nds

The "formula" for this problem is simple and should be memorized: *Any 4th or 5th in any direction, followed by a minor 2nd in any direction.*

You can now begin regular *Visualization-Improvisation* work. Use all of the problem sets from all chapters that you have studied.

Problem Sets (including other intervals already studied)

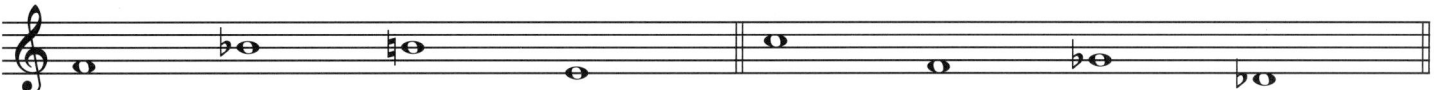

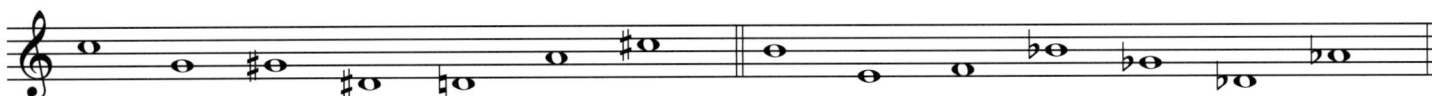

You can now begin Dictation (consult the Reference Section).

Open Pages

On the following pages you can begin to work on longer exercises. Note that these pages utilize all of the Interval Problem Sets. Practice until you can sing each whole example between checking. Use the sing-pause-sing technique!

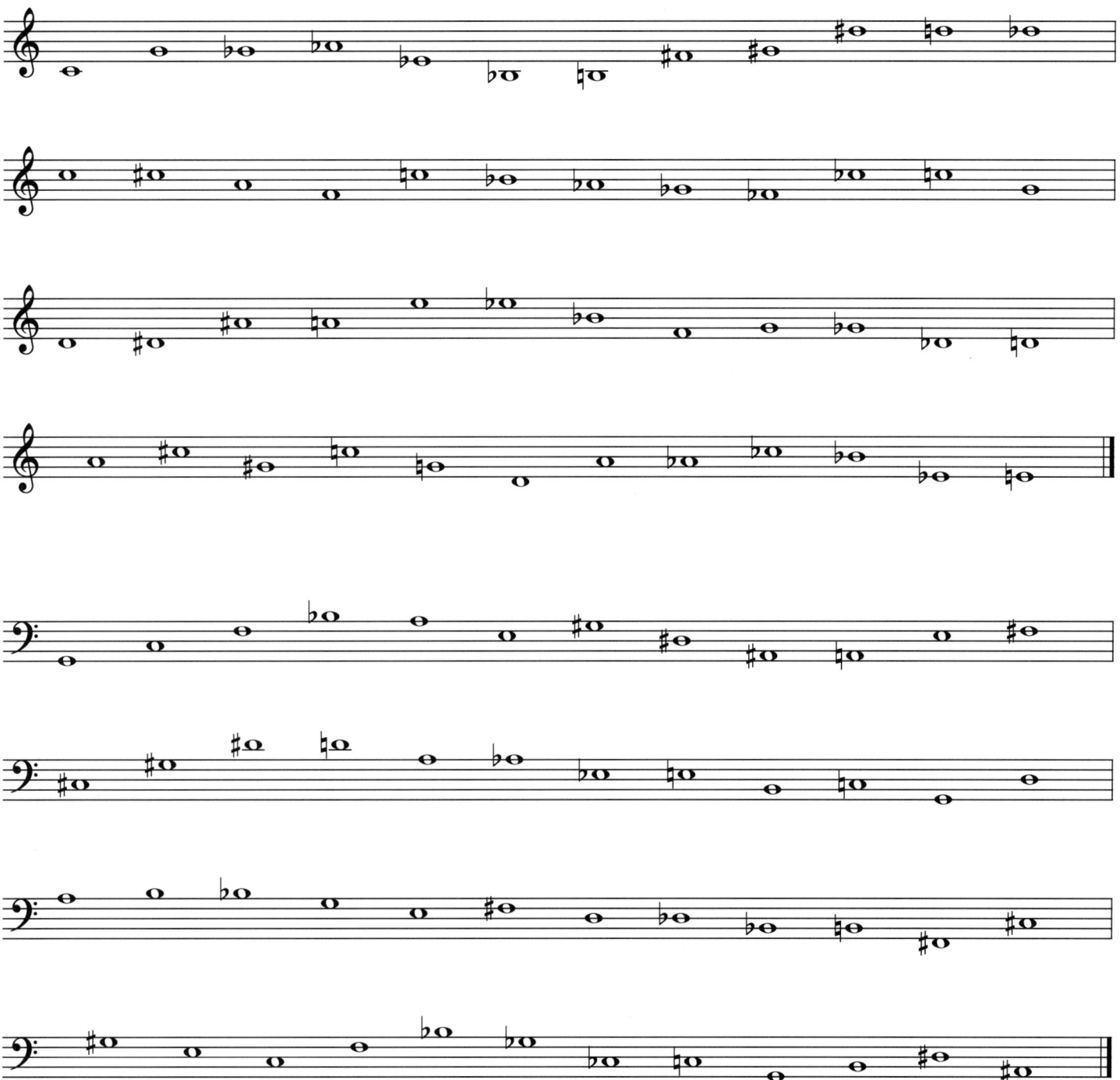

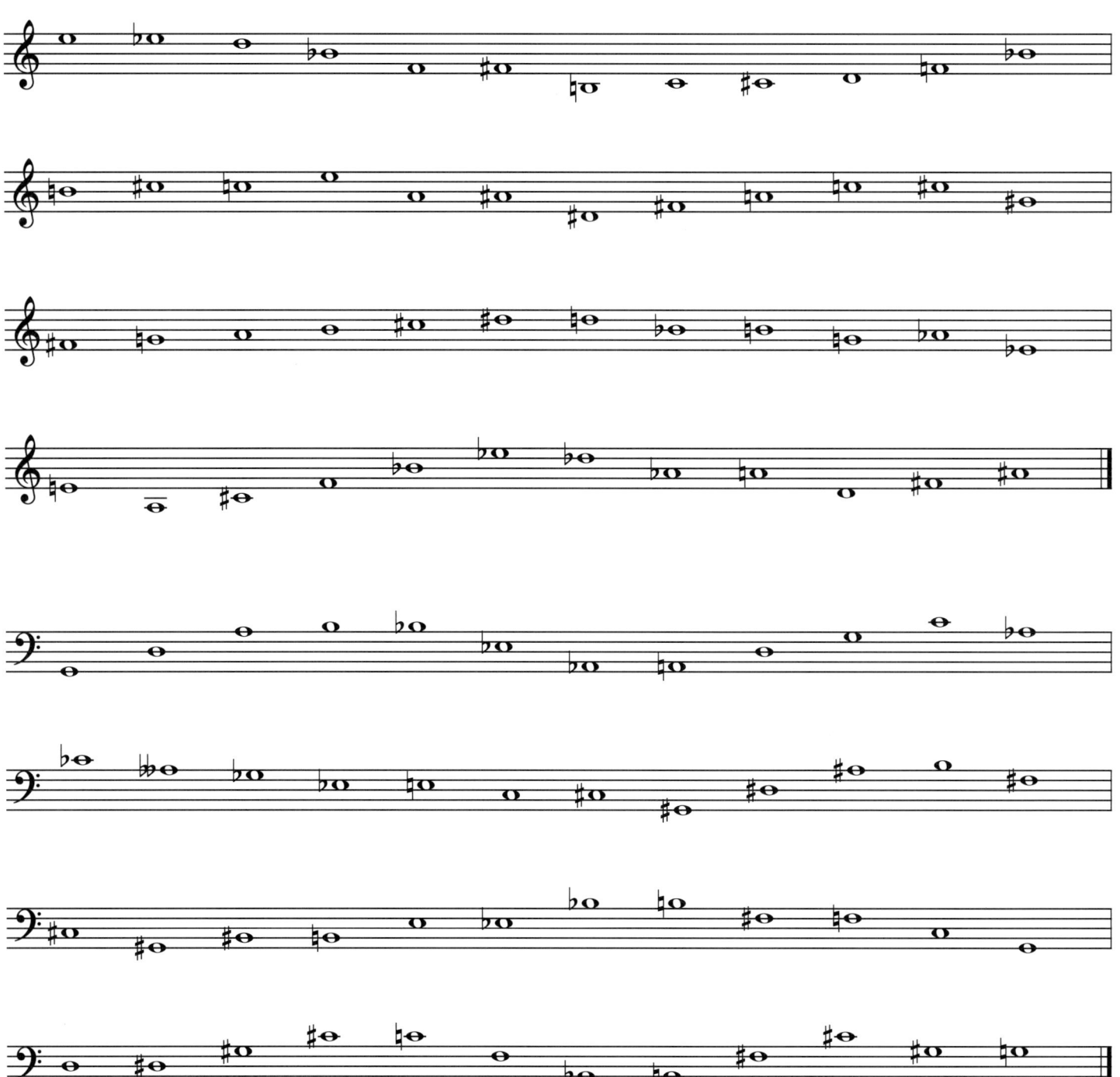

Mastery Exercises

These integrated exercises should be begun with a slow tempo (please review the Reference Chapter). Remember to sing the exercises musically!

Etudes

The tempos indicated are performance goals, so do not begin there. Choose a tempo that challenges you to know that you are singing the right notes.

CHAPTER 4 • Tritones

Preparatory Exercises

The next interval you will study is the augmented 4th or diminished 5th – commonly referred to as the *Tritone*. The Preparatory Exercises for this interval should be used for *Sight Recognition* purposes and then to master the sing-pause-sing technique. The following Building Block example will use intervals that you already know to help you build Tritones.

Using the Building Block

- Play an "F" reference pitch
- Sing the note, check intonation and stop
- Look at the next pitch, "A" natural
- Form the sound, then sing
- Look at the next pitch, "B"
- Form the sound and sing
- Work back and forth between the 3 pitches
- Become aware of the outer interval, "F" up to "B"
- Continuing, stop singing the middle note "A"

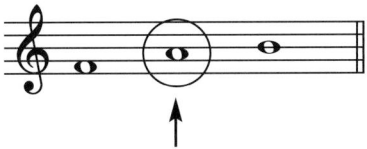

The building block, A natural

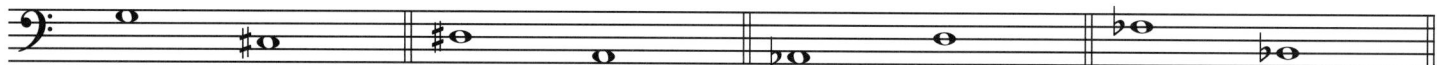

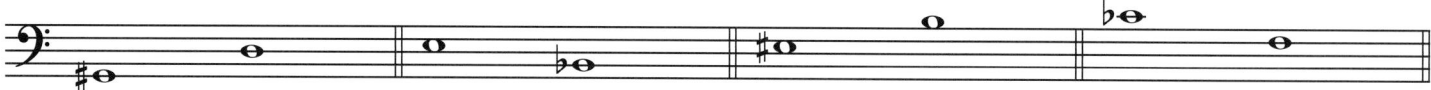

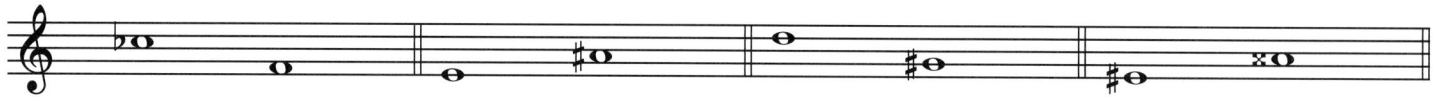

Interval Problem Exercises

The following three problem sets should be mastered one at a time before moving on to the "Open Exercises". Remember to utilize the sing-pause-sing technique that is described in the Reference Section. It is essential to your progress that you do so.

Also remember to use a *Building Block* whenever you need to.

Tritone & Perfect 4th

Tritone & Perfect 5th

Combined

You can now begin regular Visualization-Improvisation work. Use all of the problem sets from all chapters that you have studied.

INTERVALLIC EAR TRAINING

Problem Sets

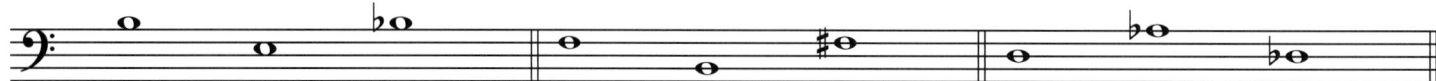

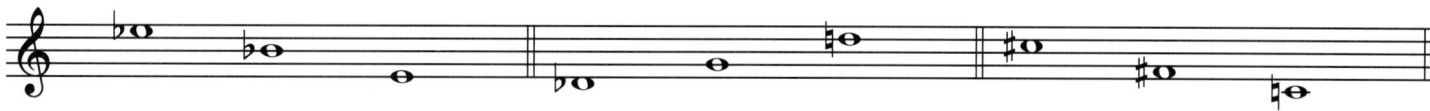

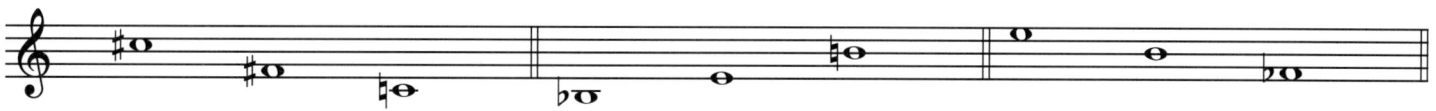

INTERVALLIC EAR TRAINING

Problem Sets (Tritones including other intervals already studied)

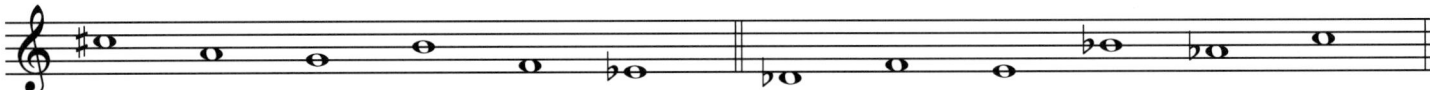

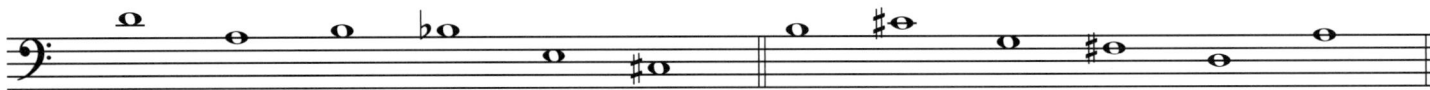

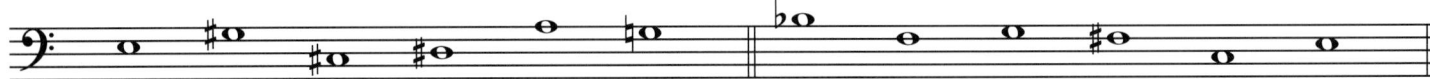

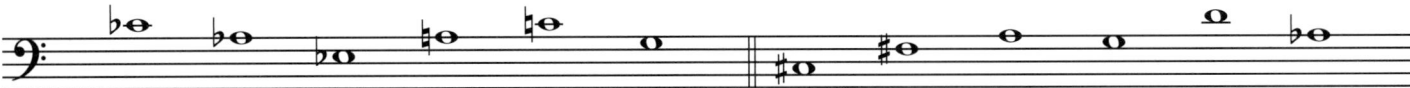

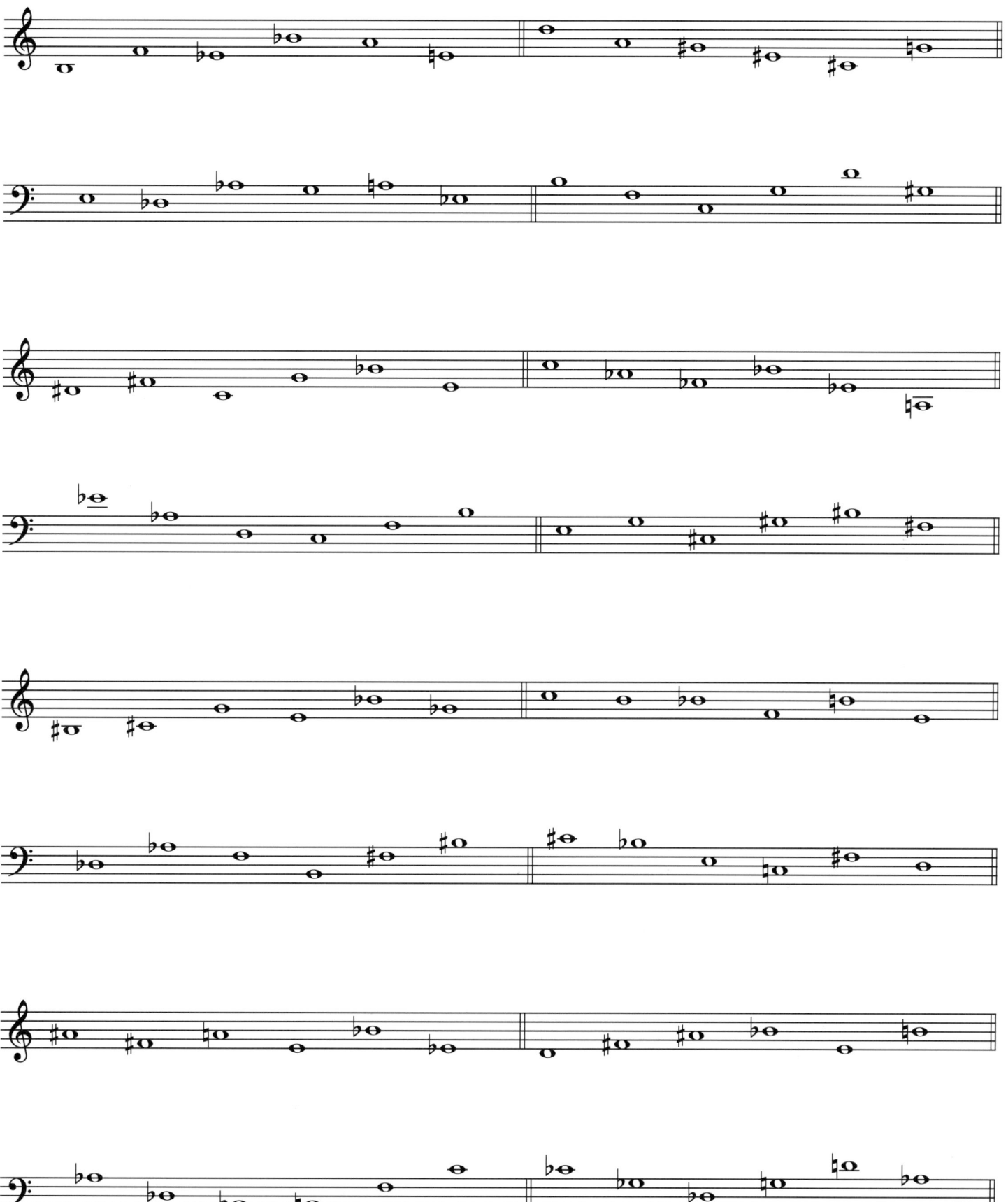

You can now begin Dictation (consult the Reference Section).

INTERVALLIC EAR TRAINING

Open Pages

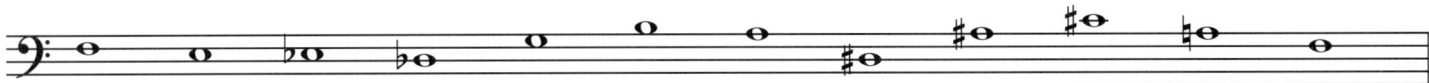

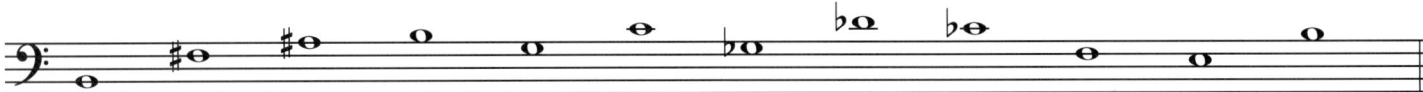

CHAPTER 4 • Tritones

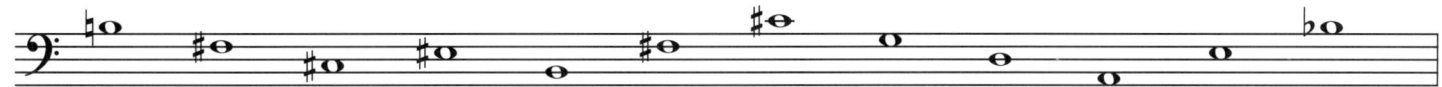

INTERVALLIC EAR TRAINING

Mastery Exercises

CHAPTER 4 • Tritones

71

Etudes

CHAPTER 5 · 6ths

Preparatory Exercises

The next interval set you will study contains minor and major 6ths. The Preparatory Exercises for these intervals should be used for *Sight Recognition* purposes and then to master the sing-pause-sing technique. The following Building Block example will use intervals that you already know to help you build 6ths.

Using the Building Block

- Play a "C" reference pitch
- Sing the note, check intonation and stop
- Look at the next pitch, "G" natural
- Form the sound, then sing
- Look at the next pitch, "A♭"
- Form the sound and sing
- Work back and forth between the 3 pitches
- Become aware of the outer interval, "C" up to "A♭"
- Stop singing the middle note "G"

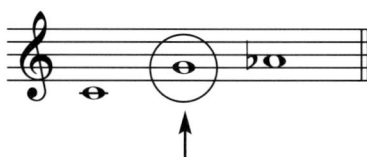

The building block, G natural

Minor 6ths

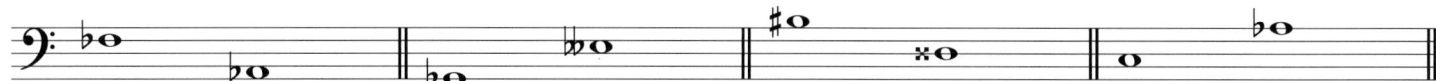

CHAPTER 5 • 6ths

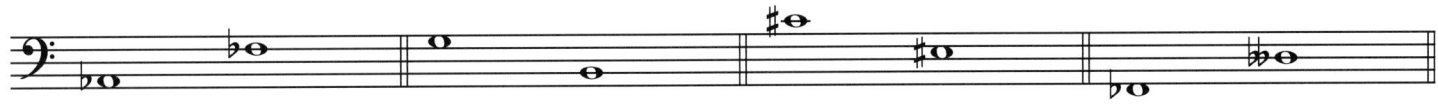
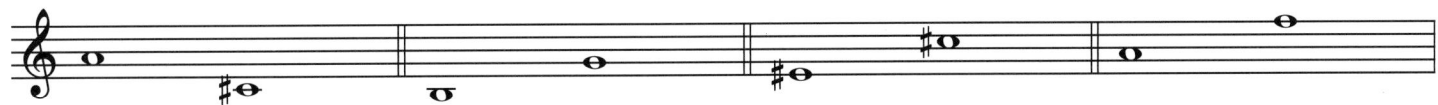

Major 6ths

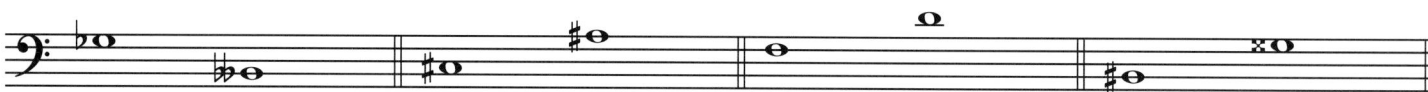
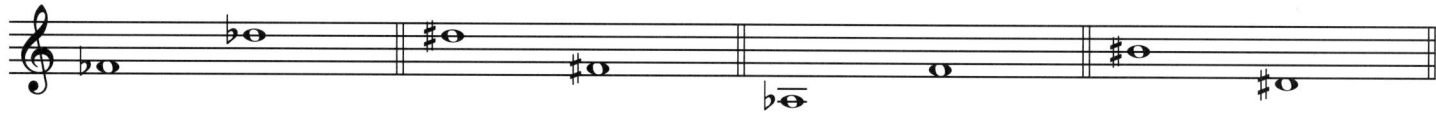

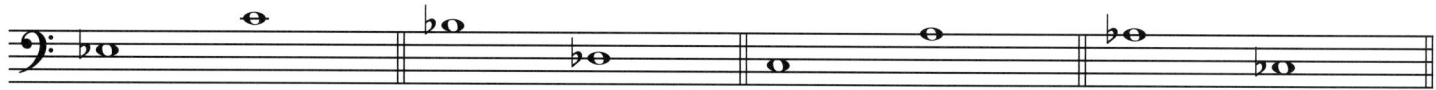

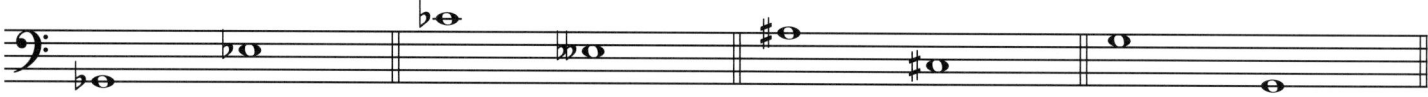

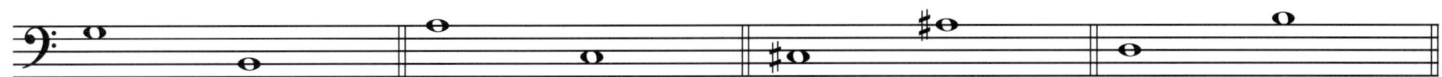

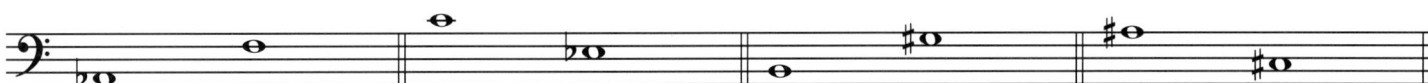
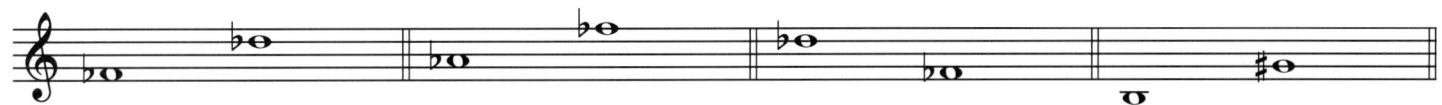

INTERVALLIC EAR TRAINING

Three-Note Sets (6ths work back and forth)

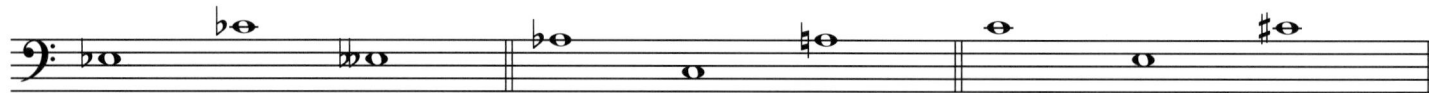

3rds and 6ths

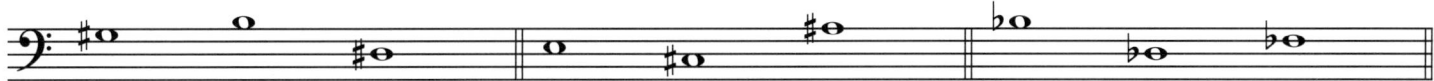

Interval Problem Exercises

The following two problem sets should be mastered before moving on to the "Open Exercises". Remember to utilize the sing-pause-sing technique that is described in the Reference Section. It is essential to your progress that you do so.

Helpful Hint on larger intervals (6ths, 7ths): You may find it useful in the initial stages of learning larger intervals to hear the inversion in your head first. For example, if you are working on an ascending major 6th, try to hear down a minor 3rd first, and then sing the higher pitch making an octave adjustment.

Also remember to use a *Building Block* whenever you need to.

Minor 6th

Minor 6th, Minor 3rd

Major 6ths

Major 3rd, Major 6th

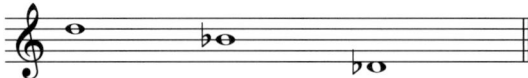

Combined

The "formula" for this problem is simple and should be memorized:

minor-minor, major-major, meaning: minor 3rd, minor 6th; minor 6th, minor 3rd; major 3rd, major 6th, and major 6th, major 3rd, all both up and down.

You can now begin regular *Visualization-Improvisation* work. Use all of the problem sets from all chapters that you have studied.

Problem Sets (including other intervals already studied)

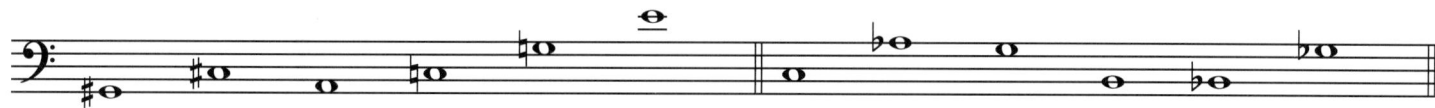

INTERVALLIC EAR TRAINING

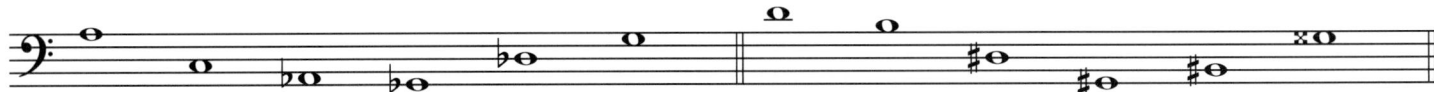

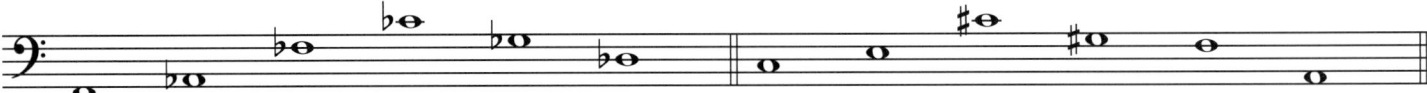

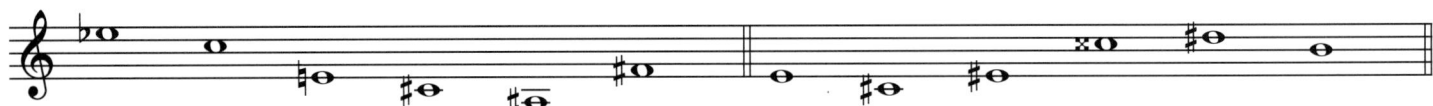

You can now begin Dictation (consult the Reference Section).

Open Pages

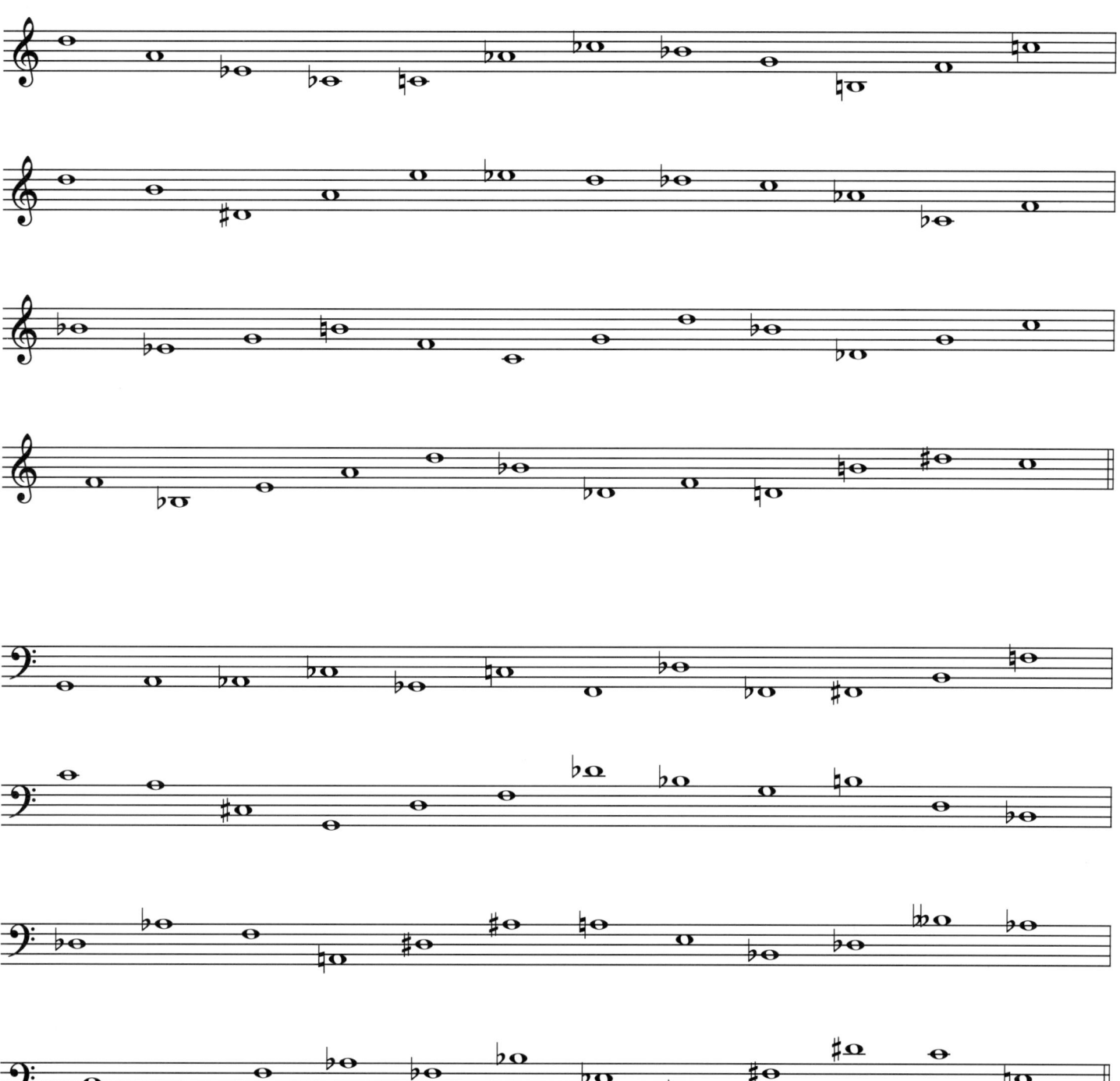

INTERVALLIC EAR TRAINING

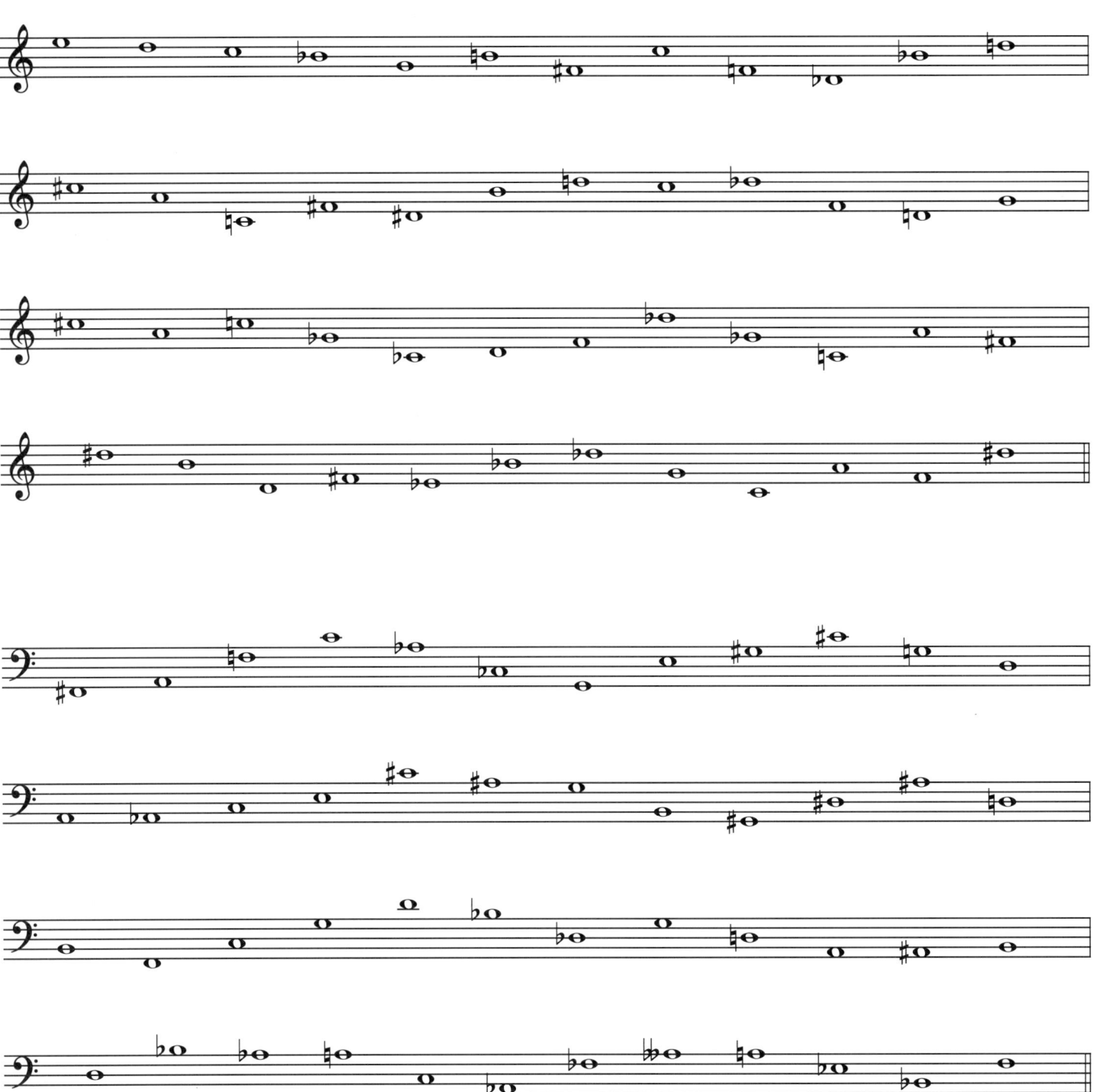

Mastery Exercises

Etudes

CHAPTER 6 • 7ths

Preparatory Exercises

The next interval set you will study contain Minor and Major 7ths. The Preparatory Exercises for these intervals should be used for *Sight Recognition* purposes and then to master the sing-pause-sing technique. The following Building Block example will use intervals that you already know to help you build 7ths.

Using the Building Block

- Play a "D" reference pitch
- Sing the note, check intonation and stop
- Look at the next pitch, "B" natural
- Form the sound, then sing
- Look at the next pitch, "C"
- Form the sound and sing
- Work back and forth between the 3 pitches
- Become aware of the outer interval, "D" up to "C"
- Continuing, stop singing the middle note "B"

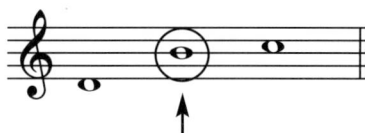

The building block, B natural

Minor 7ths

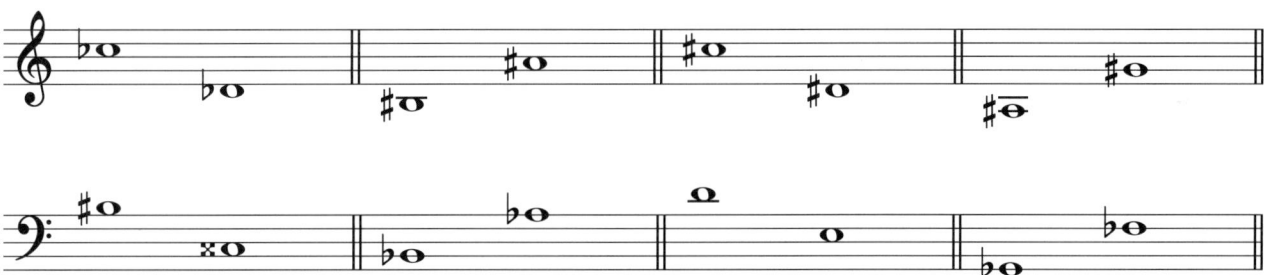

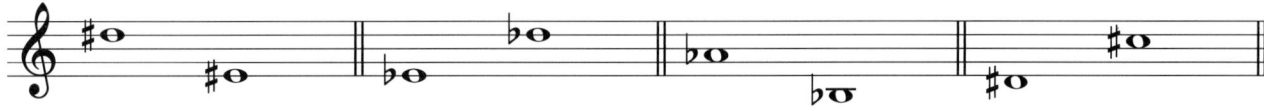

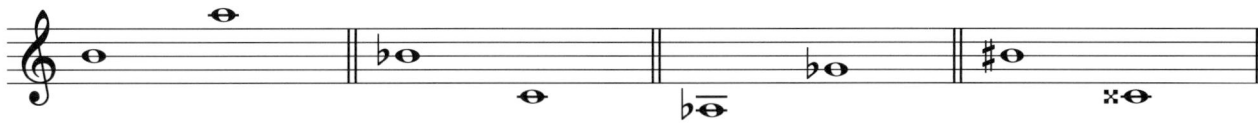

Major 7ths

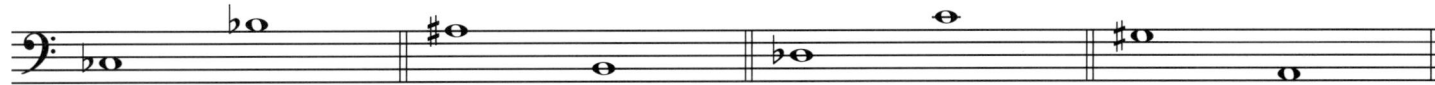

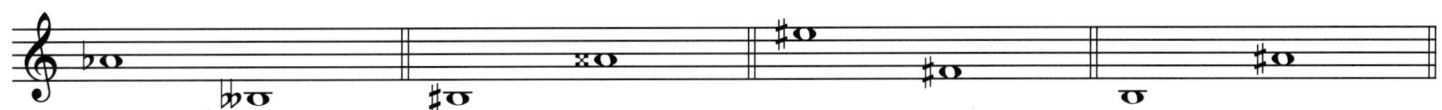

INTERVALLIC EAR TRAINING

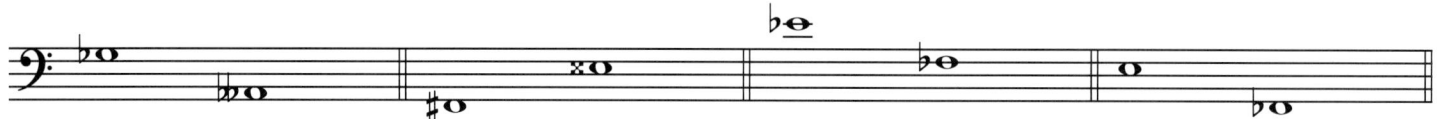
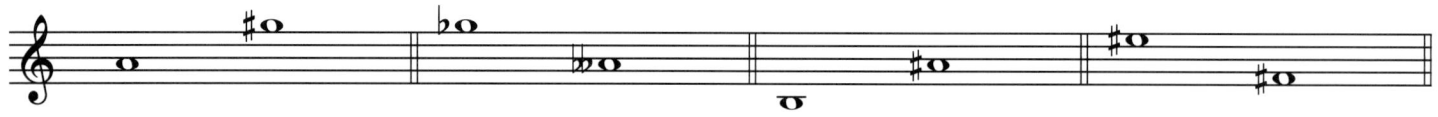

Three-Note Sets

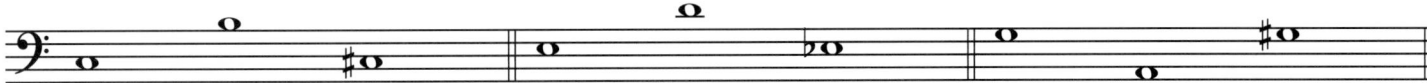

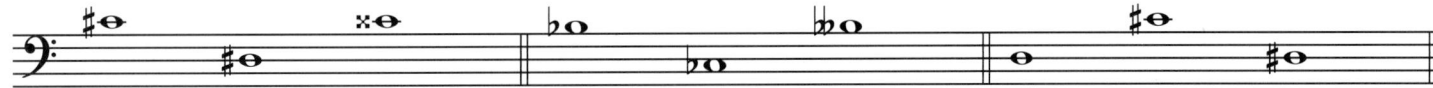

INTERVALLIC EAR TRAINING

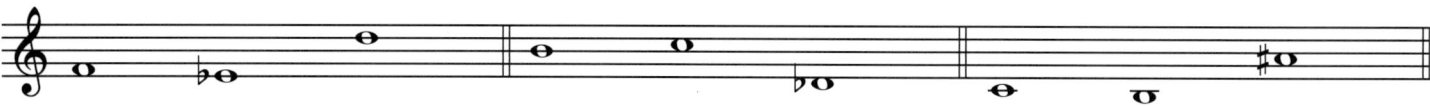

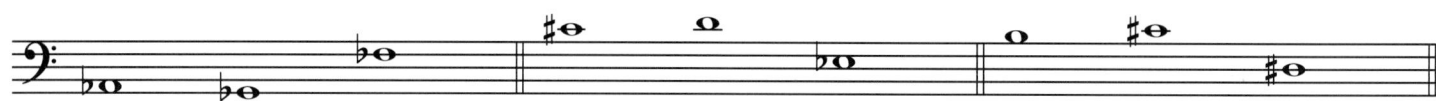

Interval Problem Exercises

The following three problem sets should be mastered one at a time before moving on to the "Open Exercises". Remember to utilize the sing-pause-sing technique that is described in the Reference section. It is essential to your progress that you do so.

Helpful Hint on larger intervals (6ths, 7ths): You may find it useful in the initial stages of learning larger intervals to hear the inversion in your head first. For example, if you are working on a descending minor 7th, try to hear up a major 2nd first, and then sing the lower pitch making an octave adjustment.

Also remember to use a Building Block whenever you need to.

Remember to use the technique outlined in the *Reference Section*.

Minor 7ths

Minor 7th, minor 2nd

Major 7ths

Major 7ths, major 2nd

Combined

The "formula" for this problem is simple and should be memorized: *"minor-minor, major-major,"* meaning: *minor 2nd, minor 7th; minor 7th, minor 2nd; major 2nd, major 7th, and major 7th, major 2nd, all both up and down.*

You can now begin regular visualization-improvisation work. Use all of the problem sets from all chapters that you have studied.

INTERVALLIC EAR TRAINING

Problem Sets (including other intervals already studied)

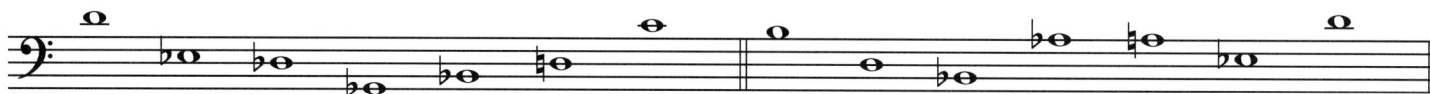

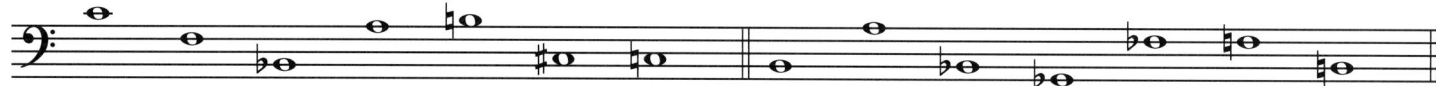

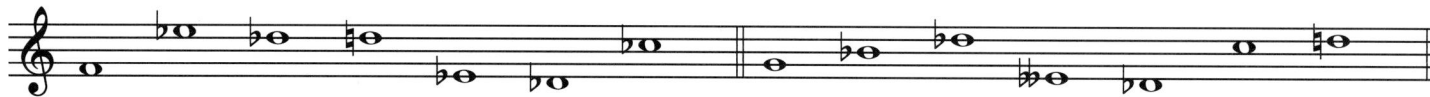

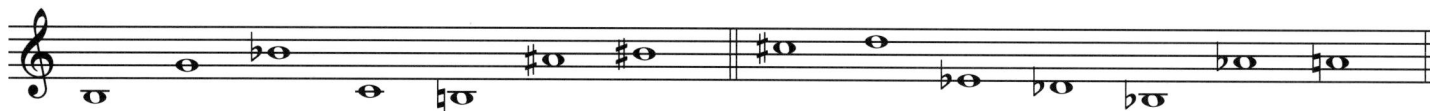

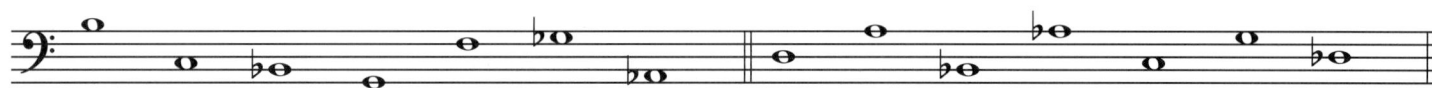

You can now begin Dictation (consult the Reference Section).

INTERVALLIC EAR TRAINING

Open Pages

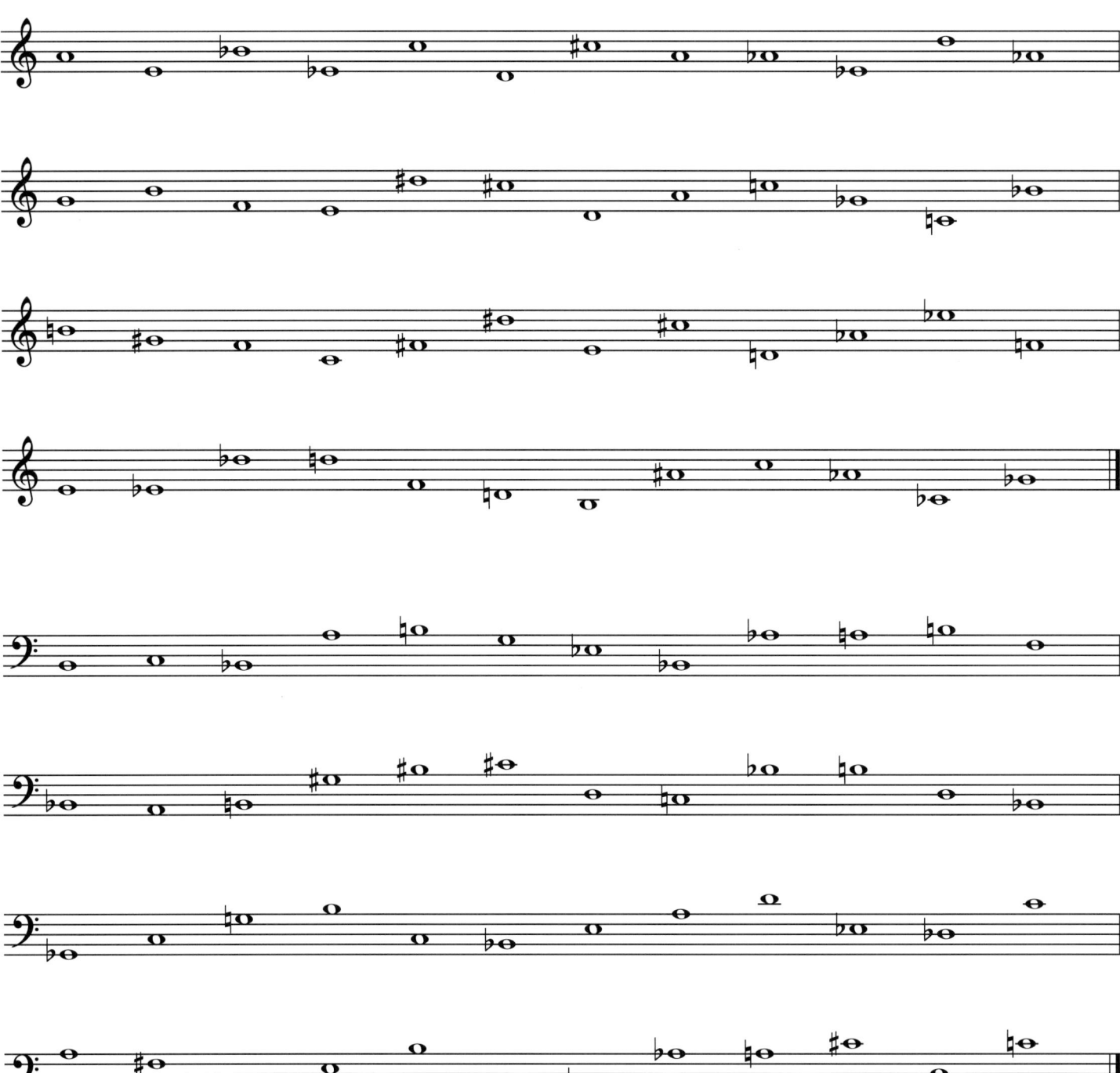

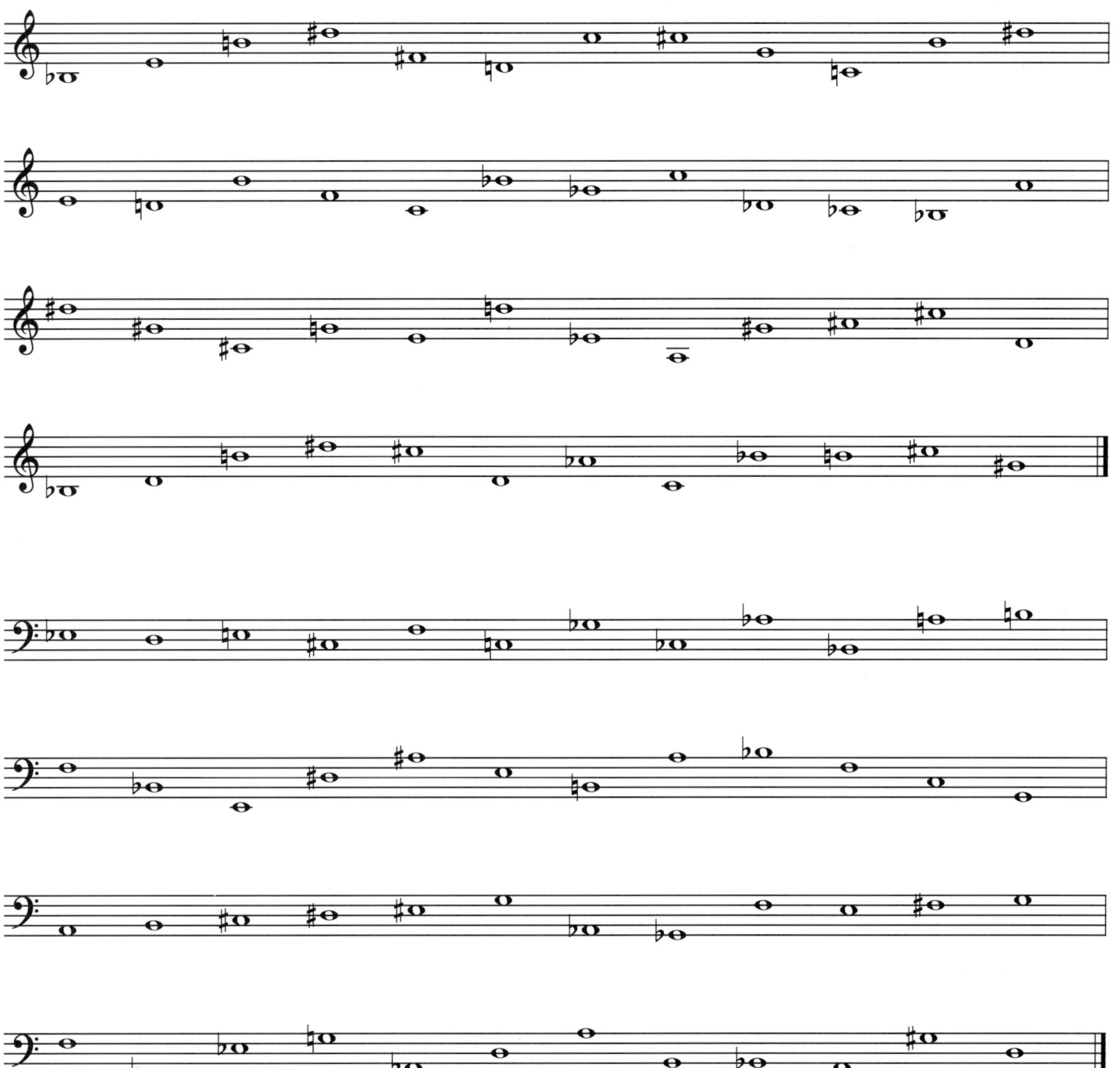

Mastery Exercises

Etudes

The tempos indicated are performance goals, so do not begin there. Choose a tempo that challenges you to know that you are singing the right notes.

CHAPTER 7 • Dictation

List of Exercises

2nds

CD1	Example	Type	Reference	Notes	Answer Page
1	1	Add-a-note	𝄞 F	7	110
2	2	Add-a-note	𝄞 B	10	110
3	3	Add-a-note	𝄢 A♭	10	110
4	4	Add-a-note	𝄞 C	15	110
5	5	Add-a-note (In 2 parts)	𝄞 F	26	110
6	6	Line	𝄞 E	6	110
7	7	Line	𝄢 G	8	110
8	8	Line	𝄞 D♭	10	110
9	9	Line	𝄞 F	7	111
10	10	Line	𝄞 C	6	111
11	11	Line	𝄢 B♭	9	111
12	12	Line	𝄞 D♭	9	111
13	13	Line	𝄢 D	12	111
14	14	Line	𝄞 C♯	12	111
15	15	Harmony	𝄞 C (B)	2	111
16	16	Harmony	𝄞 G (B)	2	111
17	17	Harmony	𝄞 A♯ (T)	2	111
18	18	Harmony	𝄢 B (B)	2	111
19	19	Harmony	𝄢 B♭ (T)	2	111
20	20	Harmony	𝄢 G (T)	3	111
21	21	Harmony	𝄞 C (M)	3	111
22	22	Harmony	𝄞 A♭ (T)	3	111
23	23	Harmony	𝄞 E (B)	3	111

3rds

CD1	Example	Type	Reference	Notes	Answer Page
24	1	Add-a-note	𝄞 C	7	112
25	2	Add-a-note	𝄢 A	10	112
26	3	Add-a-note	𝄞 D	10	112
27	4	Add-a-note	𝄢 F	15	112
28	5	Add-a-note	𝄞 D	26	112
29	6	Line	𝄢 F	6	112
30	7	Line	𝄞 B	8	112
31	8	Line	𝄢 C	10	112
32	9	Line	𝄢 E	7	113
33	10	Line	𝄞 C	6	113
34	11	Line	𝄢 A	9	113
35	12	Line	𝄞 B♭	9	113
36	13	Line	𝄢 C	12	113
37	14	Line	𝄞 B	12	113
38	15	Harmony	𝄞 B♭ (B)	3	113
39	16	Harmony	𝄞 F (T)	3	113
40	17	Harmony	𝄞 A♯ (T)	3	113
41	18	Harmony	𝄢 D♭ (B)	3	113
42	19	Harmony	𝄢 C (T)	3	113
43	20	Harmony	𝄢 F♯ (M)	3	113
44	21	Harmony	𝄞 C♭ (T)	4	113
45	22	Harmony	𝄞 F♯ (B)	3	113
46	23	Harmony	𝄞 B♭ (T)	4	113

4ths and 5ths

CD1	Example	Type	Reference	Notes	Answer Page
47	1	Add-a-note	𝄢 D	7	114
48	2	Add-a-note	𝄞 C	10	114
49	3	Add-a-note	𝄢 G	10	114
50	4	Add-a-note	𝄢 F♯	15	114
51	5	Add-a-note (In 2 parts)	𝄞 B♭	26	114
52	6	Line	𝄢 C	6	114
53	7	Line	𝄞 F♯	8	114
54	8	Line	𝄢 E	10	114
55	9	Line	𝄞 D	7	115
56	10	Line	𝄢 B	6	115
57	11	Line	𝄞 A	9	115
58	12	Line	𝄢 E♭	9	115
59	13	Line	𝄢 E	12	115
60	14	Line	𝄞 F	12	115
61	15	Harmony	𝄢 E (B)	3	115
62	16	Harmony	𝄢 A (B)	3	115
63	17	Harmony	𝄢 G (M)	3	115
64	18	Harmony	𝄞 A♯ (B)	4	115
65	19	Harmony	𝄞 C (T)	4	115
66	20	Harmony	𝄞 C (B)	4	115
67	21	Harmony	𝄢 B♭ (T)	4	115
68	22	Harmony	𝄢 C (T)	4	115
69	23	Harmony	𝄢 C♯ (B)	4	115

Tritones

CD2	Example	Type	Reference	Notes	Answer Page
1	1	Add-a-note	𝄞 B	7	116
2	2	Add-a-note	𝄢 A	10	116
3	3	Add-a-note	𝄞 C	10	116
4	4	Add-a-note	𝄞 D♭	15	116
5	5	Add-a-note (in 2 parts)	𝄢 B	26	116
6	6	Line	𝄞 A	6	116
7	7	Line	𝄢 B♭	8	116
8	8	Line	𝄞 C	10	116
9	9	Line	𝄞 E	7	117
10	10	Line	𝄢 A	6	117
11	11	Line	𝄞 D♯	9	117
12	12	Line	𝄢 F	9	117
13	13	Line	𝄢 A♭	12	117
14	14	Line	𝄞 F	12	117
15	15	Harmony	𝄢 F (B)	3	117
16	16	Harmony	𝄢 C (B)	3	117
17	17	Harmony	𝄢 G (M)	3	117
18	18	Harmony	𝄞 B♭ (B)	3	117
19	19	Harmony	𝄞 D (T)	3	117
20	20	Harmony	𝄞 E (B)	3	117
21	21	Harmony	𝄢 D (T)	4	117
22	22	Harmony	𝄢 D♯ (T)	4	117
23	23	Harmony	𝄢 G (B)	4	117
CD2	Example	Type	Reference	Notes	Answer Page

6ths

CD2	Example	Type	Reference	Notes	Answer Page
24	1	Add-a-note	𝄞 E♭	7	118
25	2	Add-a-note	𝄢 G	10	118
26	3	Add-a-note	𝄞 F	10	118
27	4	Add-a-note	𝄞 C♯	15	118
28	5	Add-a-note (in 2 parts)	𝄢 D	26	118
29	6	Line	𝄞 D	6	118
30	7	Line	𝄢 A♭	8	118
31	8	Line	𝄞 C♯	10	118
32	9	Line	𝄞 C	7	119
33	10	Line	𝄞 D	6	119
34	11	Line	𝄢 A	9	119
35	12	Line	𝄢 D♯	9	119
36	13	Line	𝄞 F	12	119
37	14	Line	𝄞 D♭	12	119
38	15	Harmony	𝄢 E (B)	3	119
39	16	Harmony	𝄢 B♭ (B)	3	119
40	17	Harmony	𝄢 C (M)	3	119
41	18	Harmony	𝄞 C♯ (B)	3	119
42	19	Harmony	𝄞 E♭ (T)	4	119
43	20	Harmony	𝄞 A (B)	4	119
44	21	Harmony	𝄢 D (T)	4	119
45	22	Harmony	𝄢 G (B)	5	119
46	23	Harmony	𝄢 F (B)	5	119

7ths

CD2	Example	Type	Reference	Notes	Answer Page
47	1	Add-a-note	𝄞 B♭	7	120
48	2	Add-a-note	𝄞 D	10	120
49	3	Add-a-note	𝄢 B	10	120
50	4	Add-a-note	𝄢 C	15	120
51	5	Add-a-note (in 2 parts)	𝄞 G	26	120
52	6	Line	𝄞 D♭	6	120
53	7	Line	𝄢 C	8	120
54	8	Line	𝄞 E	10	120
55	9	Line	𝄢 C♯	7	121
56	10	Line	𝄞 C	6	121
57	11	Line	𝄢 A	9	121
58	12	Line	𝄢 A♭	9	121
59	13	Line	𝄞 B	12	121
60	14	Line	𝄞 E	12	121
61	15	Harmony	𝄢 A (B)	3	121
62	16	Harmony	𝄢 D (B)	3	121
63	17	Harmony	𝄢 F♯ (M)	3	121
64	18	Harmony	𝄢 B (B)	3	121
65	19	Harmony	𝄢 C♯ (T)	4	121
66	20	Harmony	𝄢 G♭ (B)	4	121
67	21	Harmony	𝄞 B♭ (B)	4	121
68	22	Harmony	𝄞 A (T)	4	121
69	23	Harmony	𝄞 C (B)	5	121

Answers

CHAPTER 1 • 2nds

1.

2.
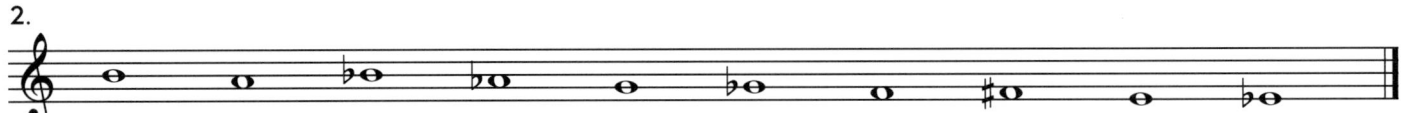

3.

4.

5.
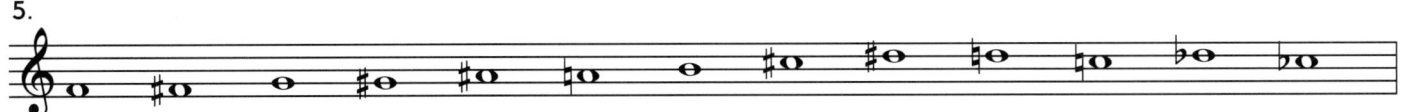

6.

7.

8.

9.

10.

11.
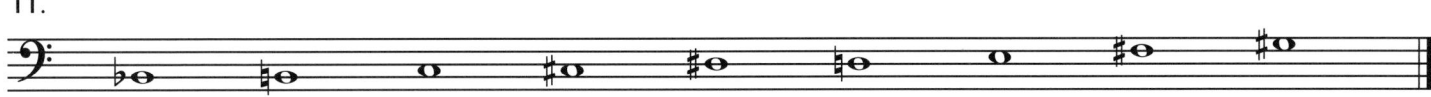

12.

13.
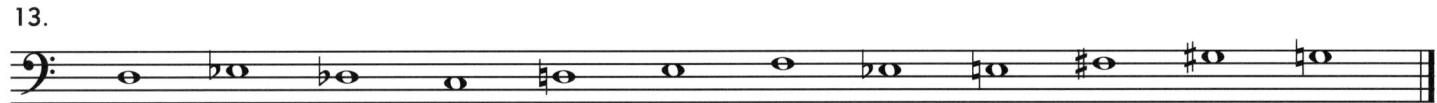

14.

15. 16. 17.
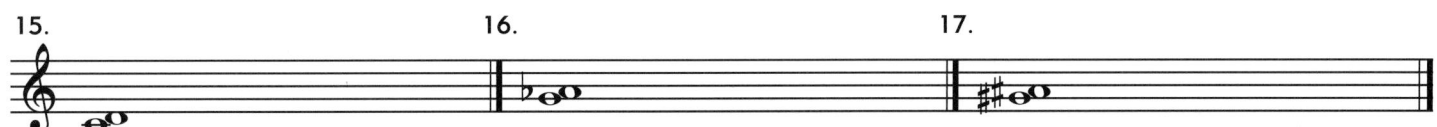

18. 19. 20.
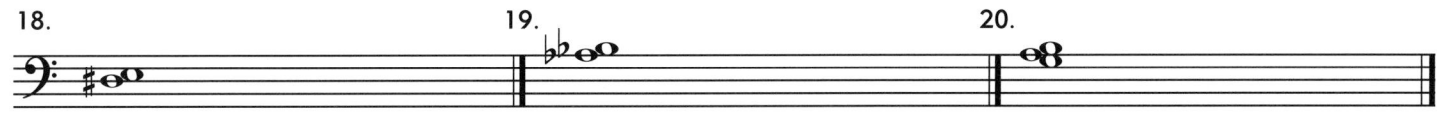

21. 22. 23.
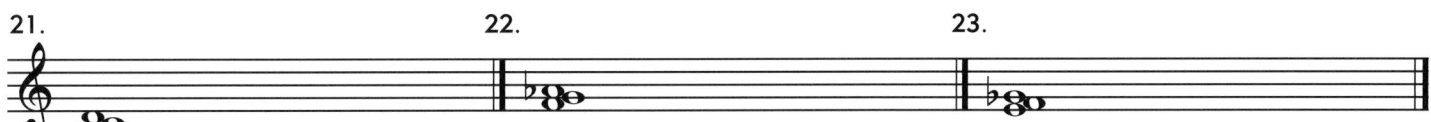

CHAPTER 2 • 3^{rds}

1.

2.

3.
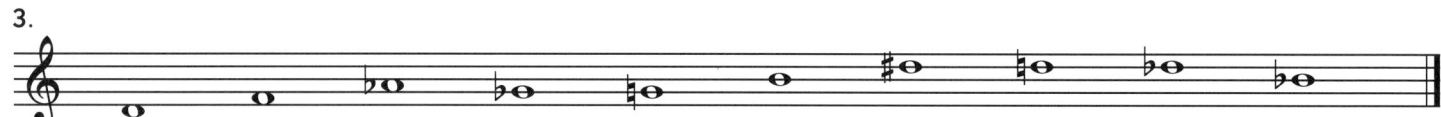

4.

5.
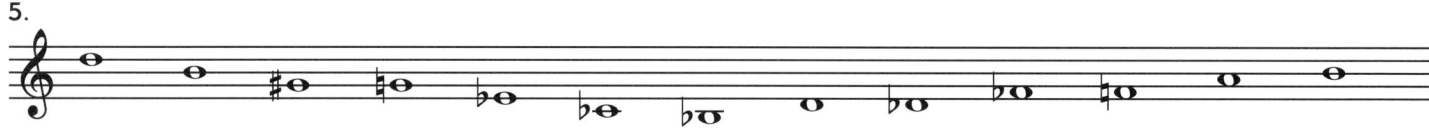

6.
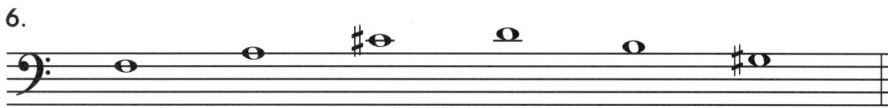

7.

8.
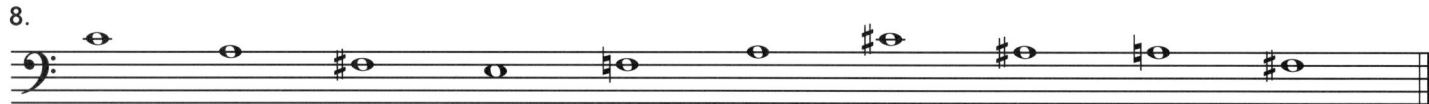

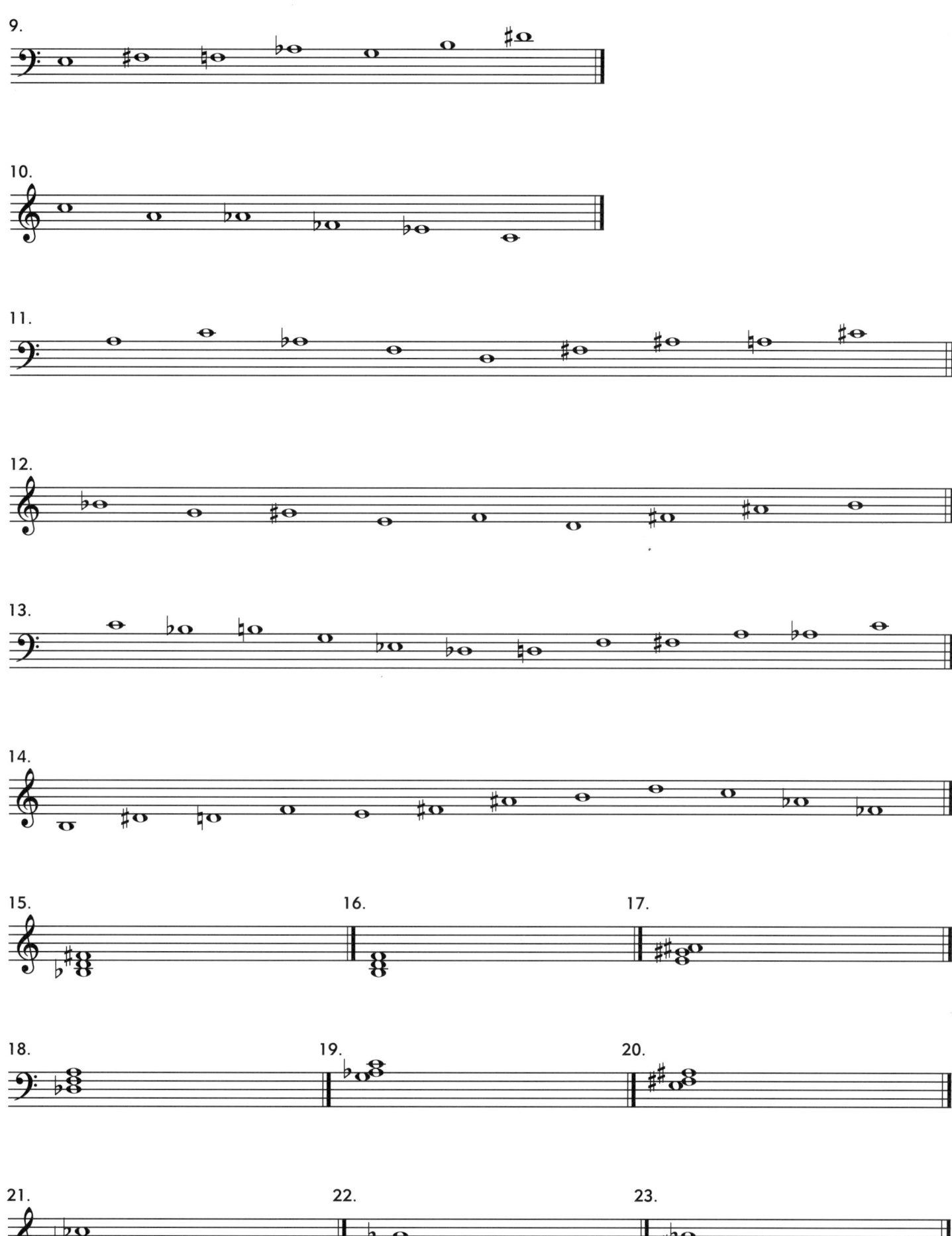

CHAPTER 3 • Perfect 4ths and 5ths

1.

2.

3.
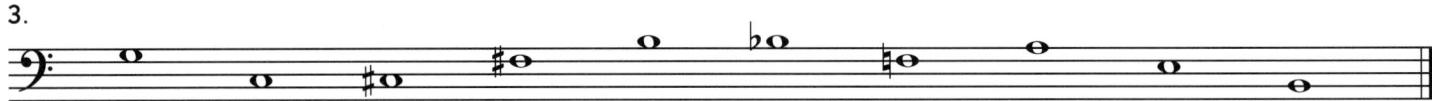

4.

5.
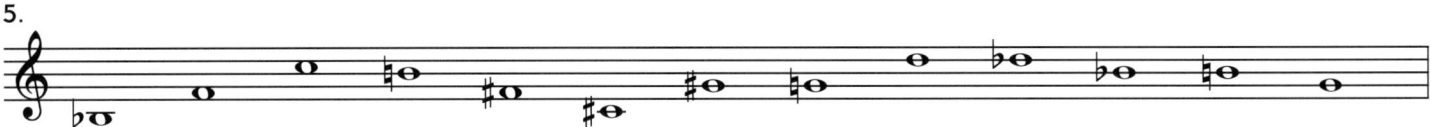

6.

7.

8.
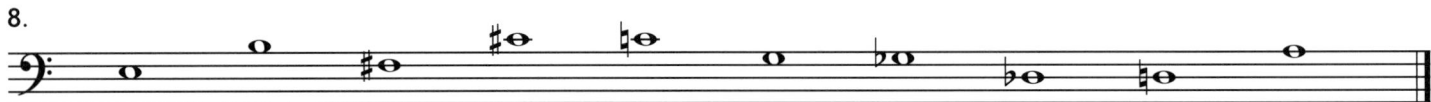

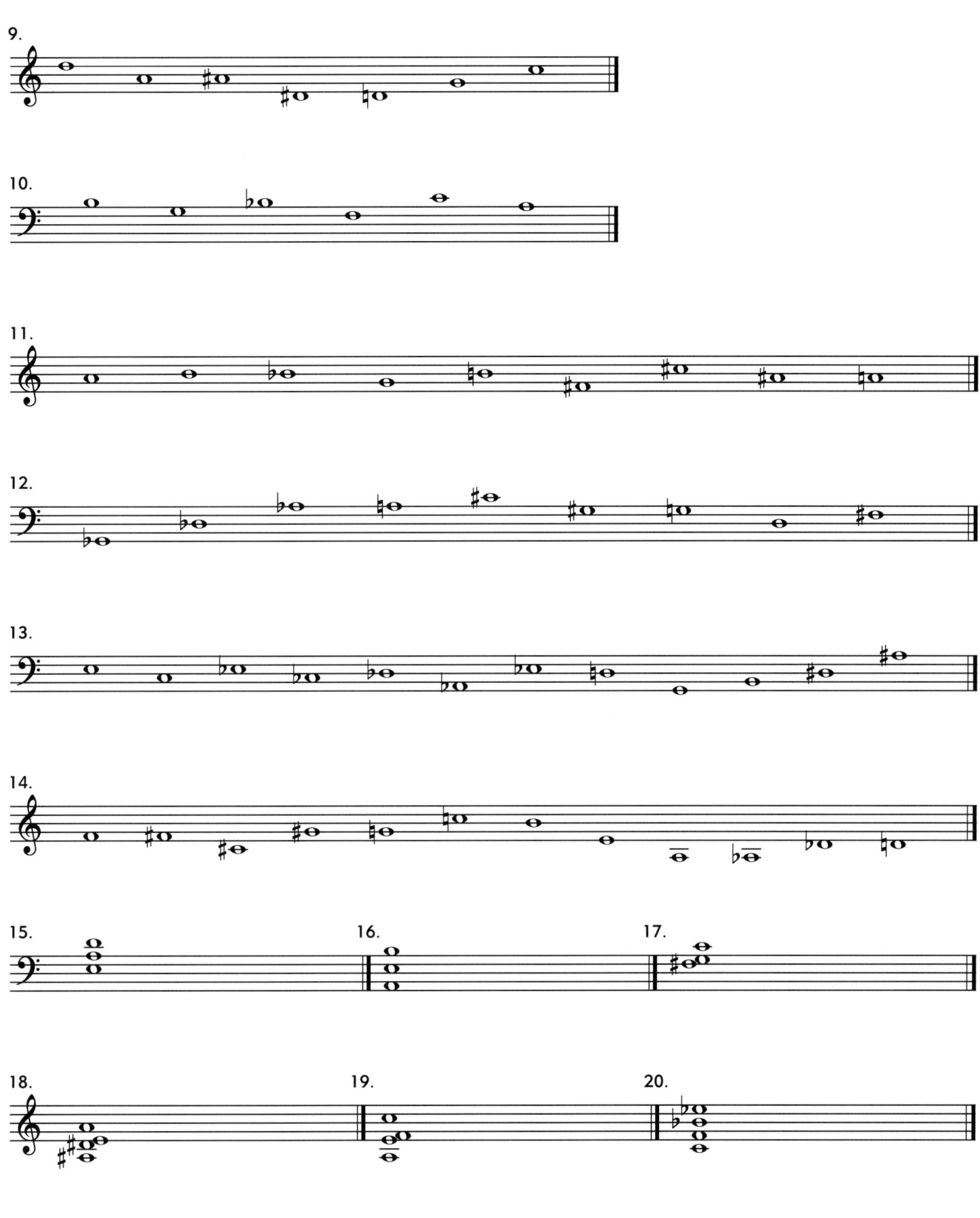

CHAPTER 4 • Tritones

1.

2.
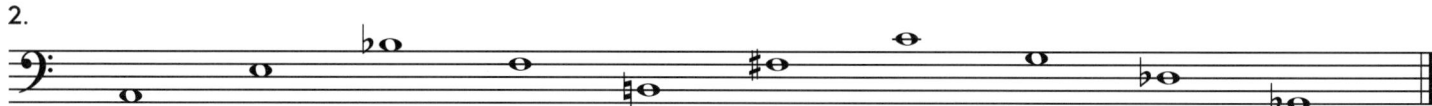

3.

4.
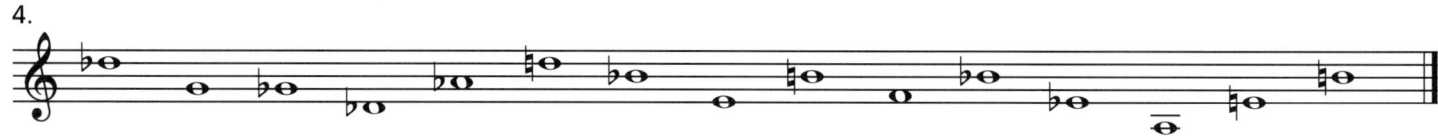

5.

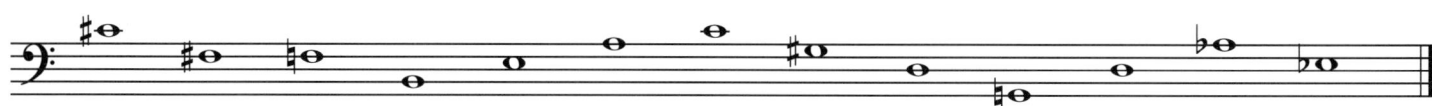

6.

7.
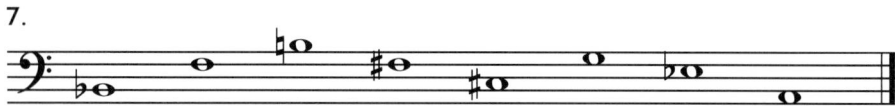

8.

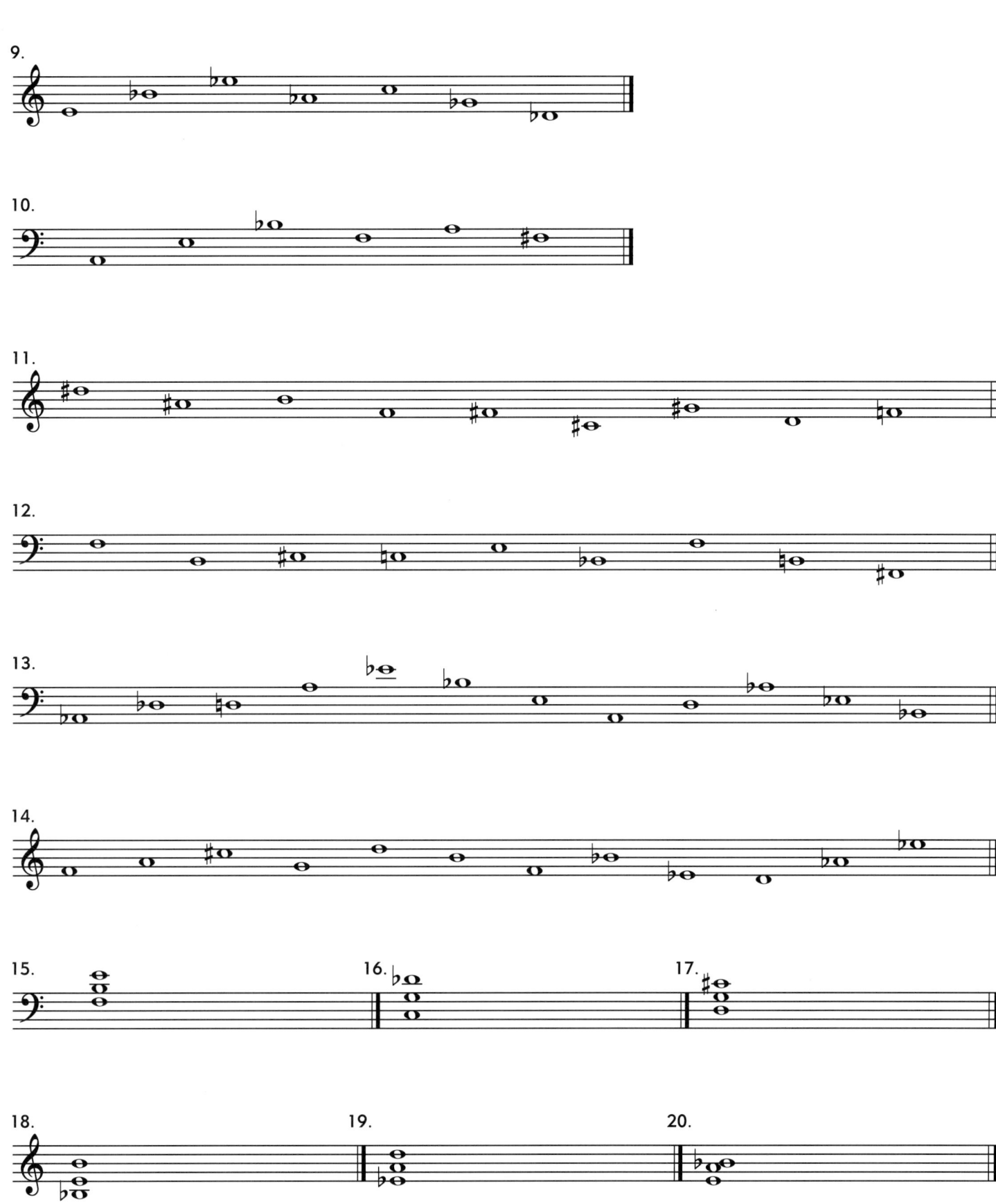

CHAPTER 5 • 6ths

1.
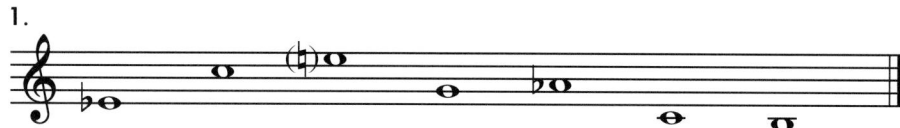

2.
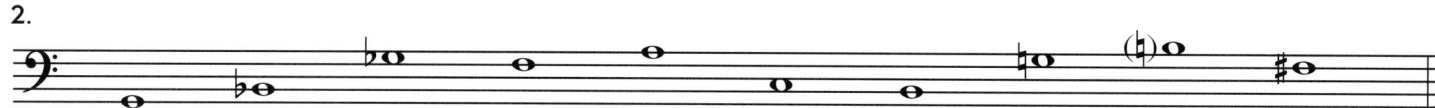

3.

4.
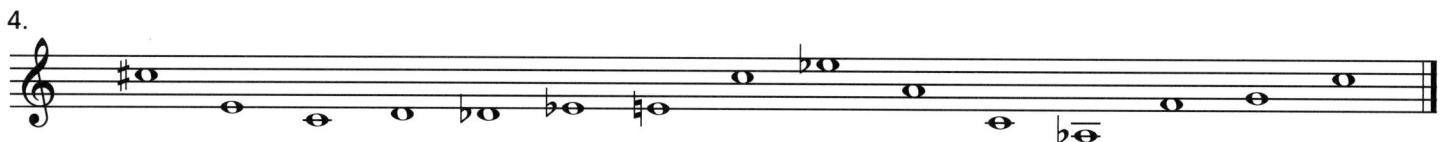

5.

6.

7.
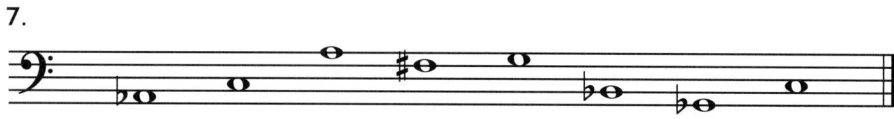

8.

9.

10.

11.

12.

13.

14.

15. 16. 17.

18. 19. 20.

21. 22. 23.

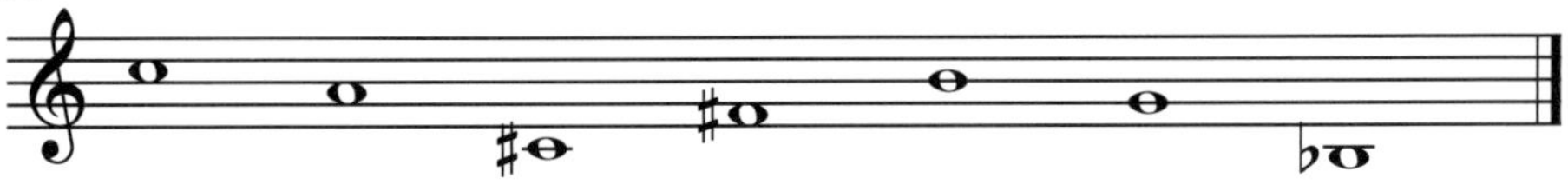

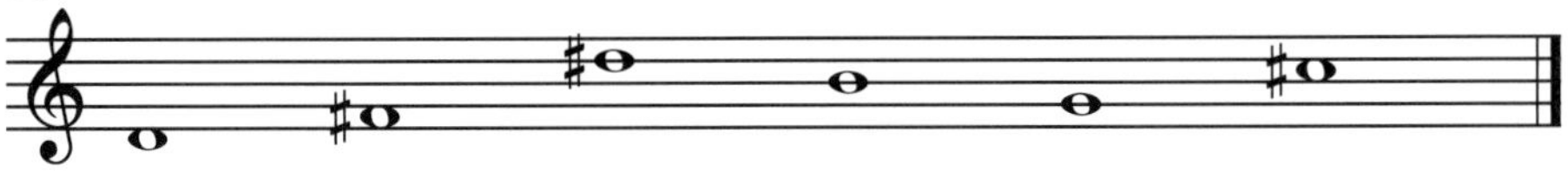

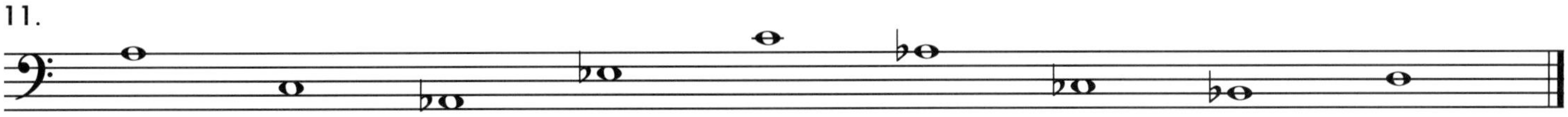

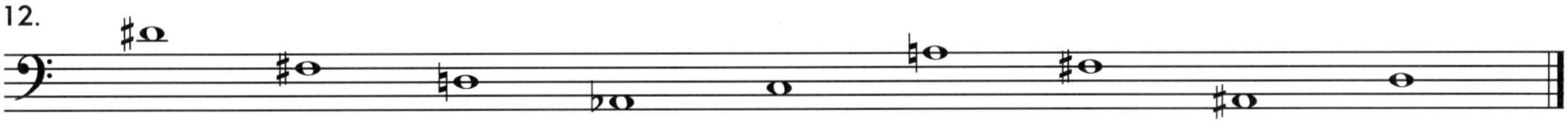

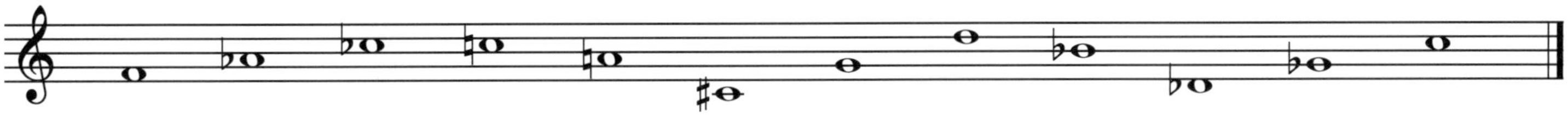

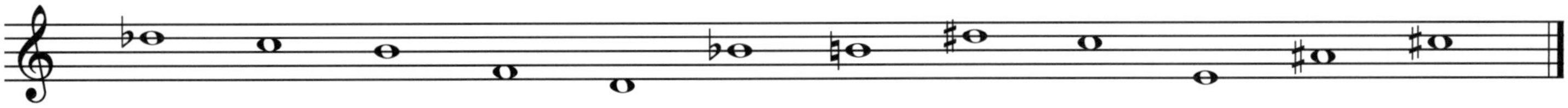

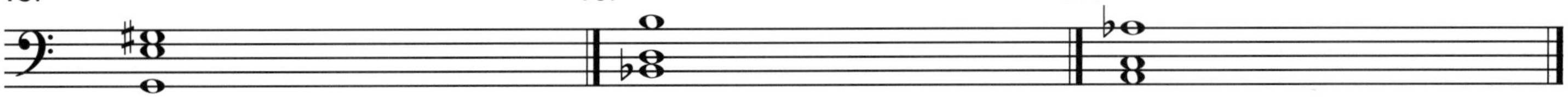

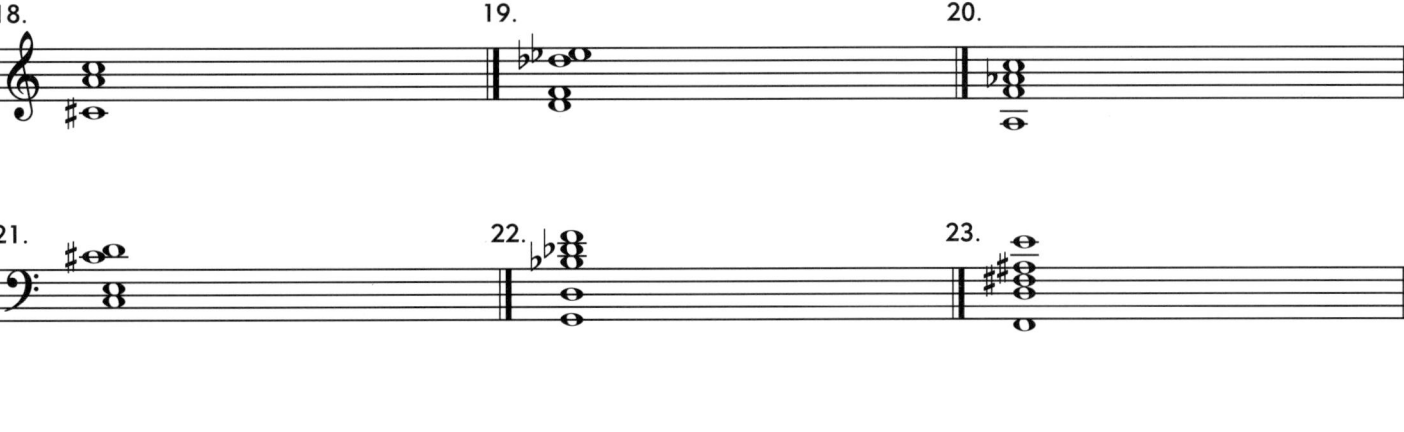

CHAPTER 6 • 7ths

1.

2.

3.

4.
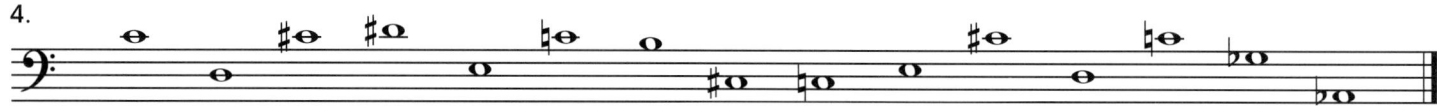

5.
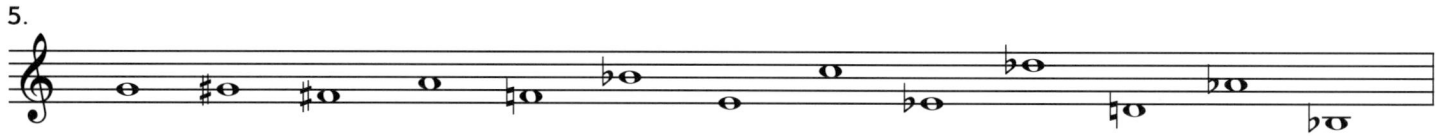

6.

7.

8.

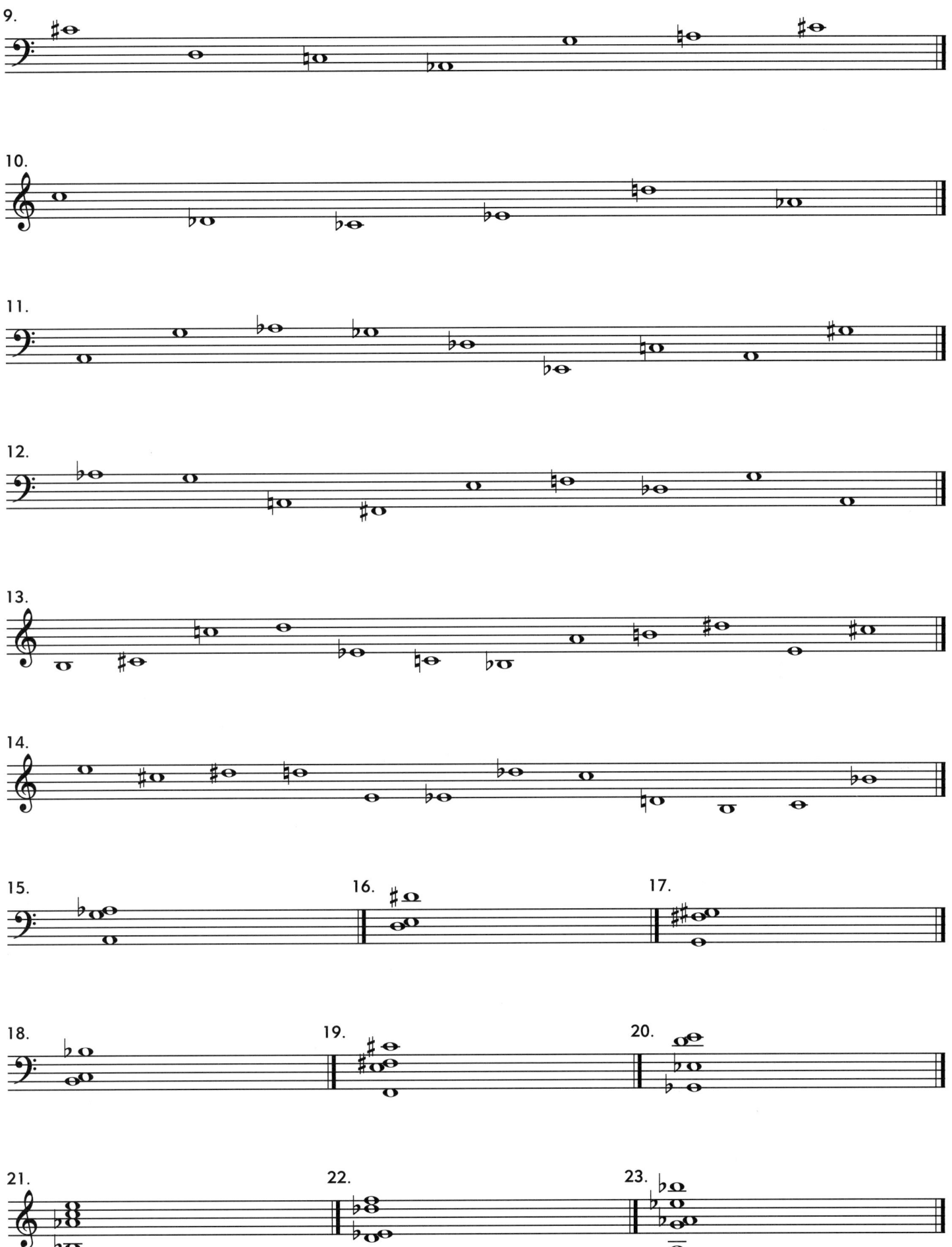

About the Author

Steve Prosser is Professor at Berklee College of Music in Boston, where he teaches Ear Training and Harmony. He is an active pianist, singer, composer, arranger, clinician and has authored many musical titles.

Prosser earned a Ph.D. from Boston College, a J.D. from Suffolk University Law School and is a member of the Massachusetts Bar.